THE THEORY OF INTERNATIONAL TRADE

The Theory of International Trade

Dr ALI M. EL-AGRAA

CROOM HELM
London & Canberra
ST. MARTIN'S PRESS
New York

© 1983 Ali M. El-Agraa
Croom Helm Ltd, Provident House, Burrell Row,
Beckenham, Kent BR3 1AT

British Library Cataloguing in Publication Data

El-Agraa, Ali M.
    The theory of international trade.
    1. Commerce
    I. Title
    382   HF1008
    ISBN (

                709909152

Library of Congress Cataloging in Publication Data

El-Agraa, A.M.
    The theory of international trade.

    Bibliogaphy: p.
    Includes indexes.
    1. International economic relations——Mathematical
models.   2. Commerce——Mathematical models. I. Title.
HF1412.E535 1983   382.1'04   83–3395
ISBN 0–312–79850–4 (St. Martin's Press)

Printed and bound in Great Britain by
Biddles Ltd, Guildford and King's Lynn

45263

CONTENTS

CONTENTS

CONTENTS

PREFACE AND ACKNOWLEDGEMENTS

The aim of this book is to use geometry as the main medium of
exposition to take those with a basic knowledge of economics
from an elementary application of that knowledge to the most
recent developments in the field of intra-industry international trade theory. This approach inevitably results in an
uneven book but there are two justifications for this. Firstly,
the incorporation of a thorough analysis of the elementary
aspects makes for a book which is more self-contained, exposit-
ionally consistent and slimmer since the approach obviates the
need for repetition which would otherwise be necessary.
Secondly, at least at this University, international trade is
taught at the second year level, hence it should be understandable that the subject cannot sensibly be taught by assuming that students fully absorb knowledge transmitted simultaneously in other fields of economics.

The inspiration of the book was the production of six
video tapes (obtainable directly from the Television Centre of
the University of Leeds) as visual aids to help my students to
an understanding of the basic tools and applications of international trade theory. This is therefore an appropriate
opportunity to thank all those who cooperated in the production
of the tapes and in particular Messrs. Nicholas N. Salmon, the
producer, and Alan B. Haigh, the graphics producer. Also, I
should like to record my gratitude to my colleague Anthony J.
Jones for a thorough reading of earlier drafts of a number of
chapters and for his incisive comments.

This being my sixth book, it is high time I expressed my
special gratitude to Diana, my wife, who is not an economist,
not only for her sympathetic and encouraging attitude to my
work but also for her thorough checking of both the style and
presentation of all my publications in the past five years.

Finally, I should like to thank Mrs. Margaret Mann of the
School of Economic Studies at the University of Leeds for her
excellent typing of the manuscript.

Leeds   A. M. E-A.

To Emeritus Professor
Arthur Joseph Brown
CBE,FBA
Teacher,Colleague,and
most of all,Friend

Chapter One

NATURE AND SIGNIFICANCE OF INTERNATIONAL DEPENDENCE

A Basic Global Macro Model

In order to understand the nature and significance of the interdependent world economy, it is helpful to consider first a simple one-country basic macroeconomic model. The following version is borrowed from Professor Wynne Godley, head of the Department of Applied Economics at Cambridge (see Godley 1981).

Godley postulates an economy measured in <u>current prices</u> so that every element expresses a money flow per unit of time such that:

$$Y \equiv G + \Delta S + PE + X - M, \qquad (1)$$

where Y is national income, G is government expenditure, ΔS is the change in the value of stocks, PE is private expenditure on both consumption and fixed investment, X is exports and M is imports.

This national income identity can be expressed as a flow of funds identity by subtracting the tax yield from both sides and rearranging:

$$G - T \equiv (Y - T - \Delta S - PE) + (M - X), \qquad (2)$$

i.e. in each period of time the <u>ex post</u> public sector deficit is, by definition, equal to the total of the private sector's net acquisition of financial assets plus (minus) the deficit (surplus) on the current account.

The tax yield (T) and the level of stocks (S) are made simple functions of Y such that:

$$T = tY, \qquad (3)$$
$$\text{and } S = \beta Y, \qquad (4)$$

where β is probably a function of interest rates. Imports are related to Y such that:

$$M = mY, \qquad (5)$$

where m is 'formally not a parameter but a variable' (Godley 1981, p.4). Because the various elements are expressed in current prices, the magnitude of m will depend not only on Y but also on the price of imports relative to the price of domestic production as well as 'other systematic factors and time trends'.

1

Nature and Significance of International Dependence

To complete the system Godley assumes the existence of equilibrium between the desired stock of financial wealth (W^*) and disposable Y such that:
$$W^* = \alpha(1 - t)\ Y, \tag{6}$$
where α is partly dependent on interest rates as well as an adjustment process given by
$$W - W_{-1} = \Phi(W^* - W_{-1}). \tag{7}$$
Substituting, one can derive the 'steady state solution' to the model:
$$Y = (G + X)/(t + m). \tag{8}$$
Equation (8) expresses a quintessential causal process relating income determination exclusively to fiscal stance measured by G/t (not by the ex post borrowing requirement $G - T$) and to trade performance measured by X/m (not by $X - M$, the ex post current balance of payments).

Assuming that borrowing from abroad must normally approximate to zero, the model suggests that fiscal policy must be conducted in such a way as to guarantee that the current account also approximates to zero. Manipulating equation (8) in this way by incorporating $X = M = mY$ it follows that a necessary and sufficient condition for achieving a zero balance of payments is that fiscal stance (measured by the term G/t) must equal trade performance (measured by X/m), since:
$$Y = G/t = X/m. \tag{9}$$
This equation suggests what role has to be played by fiscal policy in order to ensure that the balance of payments is equal to zero. It also indicates that if fiscal policy is operated subject to a balance of payments constraint, Y will be uniquely determined by trade performance.

In a two-country world (where country 2 is modelled in precisely the same manner as the above country - call it country 1), since one country's imports form the other's exports, it follows that, if the current account must remain balanced, $Y_1 = m_2 Y_2 / m_1$ and $Y_2 = m_2 Y_1 / m_2$. This tells us not only that the two countries are interdependent but that the nature and significance of this interdependence is determined by international trade.

Macroeconomics and International Trade

The above might seem a strangely arid choice of introduction to a book on the theory of international trade. However, the choice is deliberate for several reasons. Firstly, it helps to warn the reader immediately that this book is aimed at those with a basic knowledge of economics. Secondly, it stresses right from the start that international economics deals with at least two countries. Thirdly, since every country in the world is either totally dependent on or influences world trade (see the appended statistics for this and some other data on the world economy), the above model emphasizes the point that a study of economics which is not international is not worth pursuing, in spite of the claim by nation states that they are completely sovereign. Fourthly, although the above model is not adopted in this book, using it as an introduction helps to demonstrate that there are several ways of dealing with international economics. Finally, the model highlights one of the crucial assumptions used throughout the book: trade must always remain balanced.

About this Book

International economics has two main branches: international monetary economics and the theory of international trade. The former tackles the interdependent world economy in <u>monetary</u> terms, hence the above model is of direct relevance here. The latter considers the world economy in <u>real</u> terms, hence the macroeconomic model is not very useful here - being Keynesian, it ignores the supply side of the economy. This book is confined not only to the theory of international trade but to a more limited field within this since some aspects of the subject are not tackled with the same rigour as others, e.g. trade in intermediate products and intra-industry trade.

More specifically, this book tries to answer questions such as: (i) what determines the pattern and composition of international trade? (ii) do countries gain from trading? (iii) what effect does international trade have on income distribution? (iv) is there an economic rationale for protectionism? (v) why do two or more nations agree to pursue common aims and policies, i.e. why international economic integration? (vi) what is the effect of economic growth on international trade?

The book is organised in such a way that chapters 2 and 3 give a rigorous analysis of the basic tools of supply and demand utilised throughout the book. Chapter 4 brings the forces of supply and demand together to show the nature of equilibrium output determination and the gains from trade. Chapter 5 incorporates all the information gathered from chapters 2-4 to demonstrate how international prices - the terms of trade - are determined. Chapters 6 and 7 deal respectively with the theories purporting to explain the pattern and composition of international trade and the implications of the standard trade model. Chapters 8-10 tackle the problems raised by protection. The remaining chapters deal respectively with the theory of economic integration, economic growth and international trade, market imperfections and factor mobility, and economies of scale.

As suggested at the beginning of this chapter, the book is aimed at advanced British undergraduates and postgraduates taking international economics for the first time. Also, the book represents a synoptic overview of the subject into which some interesting new developments are fully incorporated for the first time. Finally, the medium of exposition is mainly geometry since it can be carried to such an extent as to explain practically any proposition without being unnecessarily involved with advanced mathematics. All these considerations make this a unique book, hence there is no need to justify the addition of yet another book on the subject.

THE WORLD ECONOMY: STATISTICAL APPENDIX

Table 1.1(a): Some Basic Indicators

GROUP	Average Annual Growth Rate (%) GNP 1960-79	GDP 1960-70	GDP 1970-79	Structure of Production: Distribution of GDP (%) Agriculture 1960	1979	Industry 1960	1979	Manufacturing 1960	1979	Services 1960	1979
1 Low-income Countries	1.6	4.5	4.7	51	34	17	36	11	13	32	30
2 Middle-income Countries:	3.8	6.1	5.5	22	14	30	38	21	24	47	48
a. Oil exporters	3.1	6.5	5.5	23	14	26	42	17	19	51	44
b. Oil importers	4.1	5.9	5.5	21	14	32	36	23	26	46	50
3 Industrial Market Economies	4.0	5.1	3.2	6	4	40	37	30	27	54	59
e.g. UK	2.2	2.9	2.1	4	2	43	36	32	25	53	62
Japan	9.4	10.5	5.2	13	5	45	42	34	30	42	53
USA	2.4	4.3	3.1	4	3	38	34	29	24	58	63
W Germany	3.3	4.4	2.6	6	2	53	49	40	38	41	44
4 Capital-surplus Oil Exporters	5.0	..	6.5	..	2	..	75	..	5	..	23
5 Non-market Industrial Economies	4.3	4.8	5.2	21	15	62	63	52	..	17	22
e.g. USSR	4.1	5.2	5.1	21	16	62	62	52	..	11	28

THE WORLD ECONOMY: STATISTICAL APPENDIX

Table 1.1(b): Some Basic Indicators

GROUP	Exports of Goods and Non-factor Services (% of GDP)		Average Annual Growth Rate (%) EXPORTS		IMPORTS		Terms of Trade (1975=100)	
	1960	1979	1960–70	1970–79	1960–70	1970–79	1960	1979
1 Low-income Countries	7	11	5.0	-1.0	5.2	3.3	113	97
2 Middle-income Countries:	16	20	5.4	4.3	6.6	5.0	100	98
a. Oil exporters	21	25	4.5	1.7	3.6	11.1	69	113
b. Oil importers	14	18	6.3	4.4	7.7	3.7	109	94
3 Industrial Market Economies	12	19	8.4	5.9	9.3	4.5	100	98
e.g. UK	21	29	4.8	8.2	5.0	4.4	112	107
Japan	11	12	17.2	9.1	13.7	4.8	150	93
USA	5	9	6.0	6.9	9.8	5.4	115	91
W Germany	19	26	10.1	6.0	10.1	6.0	90	95
4 Capital-surplus Oil Exporters	..	65	8.2	-2.0	10.8	18.0	26	118
5 Non-market Industrial Economies	..	..	9.0	7.5	7.9	7.6	..	..
e.g. USSR	..	..	9.7	7.3	7.1	9.6	..	..

Table 1.2: Structure of Merchandise Exports (Percentage share of Merchandise Exports)

GROUP	Fuels, Minerals and Metals		Other Primary Commodities		Textiles and Clothing		Machinery and Transport Equipment		Other Manufactures	
	1960	1978	1960	1978	1960	1978	1960	1978	1960	1978
Low-income Countries	13	32	69	38	13	12	(.)	3	5	15
China and India	..	12	..	35	..	22	..	4	..	27
Other low-income	15	49	79	40	3	6	(.)	1	3	4
Middle-income Countries	27	35	60	29	3	9	2	12	8	17
Oil exporters	46	78	50	14	1	3	(.)	2	3	3
Oil importers	16	11	67	37	4	12	2	15	11	25
Industrial Market Economies	11	8	23	15	7	5	29	38	30	34
UK	7	9	9	10	8	5	44	37	32	39
Japan	11	2	10	2	28	4	23	57	28	35
USA	10	6	27	25	3	2	35	43	25	24
W Germany	9	6	4	6	4	5	44	47	39	36
Capital-surplus Oil Exporters	96	98	4	(.)	0	(.)	0	1	0	1
Non-market Industrial Economies	18	25	33	11	3	3	25	34	21	27
USSR	24	42	28	9	1	(.)	21	20	26	29

7

8 Table 1.3: Structure of Merchandise Imports (Percentage share of Merchandise Imports)

GROUP	Food		Fuels		Other Primary Commodities		Machinery and Transport Equipment		Other Manufactures	
	1960	1978	1960	1978	1960	1978	1960	1978	1960	1978
Low-income Countries	22	17	6	11	16	20	25	24	31	28
China and India	..	17	..	10	..	32	..	18	..	23
Other Low-income	22	18	6	12	6	6	20	30	46	34
Middle-income Countries	15	12	9	17	13	8	28	32	35	31
Oil exporters	18	16	7	6	8	5	27	42	40	31
Oil importers	14	11	10	19	16	9	29	28	31	33
Industrial Market Economies	22	13	11	19	24	10	16	25	27	33
UK	36	16	11	12	27	10	8	26	18	36
Japan	17	17	17	40	49	20	9	7	8	16
USA	24	10	10	24	25	8	10	27	31	31
W Germany	26	15	8	16	28	10	10	21	28	38
Capital-surplus Oil Exporters	..	12	..	1	..	2	..	42	..	43
Non-market Industrial Economies										
USSR	12	..	4	..	18	..	30	..	36	..

Table 1.4: Destination of Merchandise Exports (Percentage of Total)

GROUP	Industrial Market Economies 1960	1979	Developing Countries 1960	1979	Non-market Industrial Economies 1960	1979	Capital-surplus Oil Exporters 1960	1979
Low-income Countries	51	61	29	29	19	5	1	5
China and India	39	52	25	33	36	9	(.)	6
Other Low-income	63	69	33	26	3	2	1	3
Middle-income Countries	68	67	24	26	8	4	(.)	3
Oil exporters	68	73	27	26	5	1	(.)	(.)
Oil importers	68	64	23	27	9	6	(.)	3
Industrial Market Economies	67	69	30	24	3	3	(.)	4
UK	57	70	38	23	3	2	2	5
Japan	45	46	51	43	2	3	2	8
USA	61	57	37	36	1	3	1	4
W Germany	70	73	25	20	4	4	1	3
Capital-surplus Oil Exporters	83	70	16	29	1	(.)	0	1
Non-market Industrial Economies	19	..	22	..	59	..	(.)	..
USSR	18	..	31	..	51	..	(.)	..

Notes :
1. .. means not available.
2. (.) means less than half the unit shown.
3. The Groups consist of : 36 low-income developing countries with a per capita income of US $ 370 or less; 60 middle-income developing countries with a per capita income of more than US $ 370; 18 industrial market economies; 4 capital-surplus oil exporters (Iraq, Kuwait, Libya, Saudi Arabia); and 6 non-market industrial economies.

Source : <u>World Development Report 1981</u>, Oxford University Press for the World Bank.
        See the source for technical qualifications.

Chapter Two

THE ANALYSIS OF DEMAND IN INTERNATIONAL TRADE

In this chapter I shall construct methods by which one can depict a community's consumption preferences: its planned demand per period of time for the set of goods and services it is offered, at various prices, given a certain set of market circumstances.

Basic microeconomic theory shows that a single consumer's planned consumption behaviour can be analysed in terms of four basic theoretical constructs:

1. Marshallian Demand Analysis;
2. Indifference Analysis;
3. Revealed Preference Analysis; and
4. Commodities-as-Attributes Analysis.

Each of these four approaches creates certain difficulties when applied to the community as a whole as opposed to a single consumer. However, the two approaches most widely used in the theory of international trade, at this level of exposition, are the indifference and revealed preference analyses. I shall therefore discuss these two approaches in this chapter, aiming to show that the problems they raise are not only interesting in their own right but should also be of fundamental concern to any economist seriously practising the profession.

Indifference Analysis

In basic microeconomic analysis, the consumption preferences of a single consumer can be represented by a set of indifference curves - an indifference map.

Figure 2.1 shows how Diana, a consumer, expresses her consumption preferences for two broad categories of commodities, here chosen as Food on the vertical axis and Clothing on the horizontal axis - 0 is the origin for Diana. I am assuming that these two commodities either represent all agricultural and manufactured goods or that Diana's consumption of other goods remains unaffected throughout the analysis; hence the choice of these two commodities is, in a sense, arbitrary. The result is a set of indifference curves - D_1, D_2, D_3, etc. -

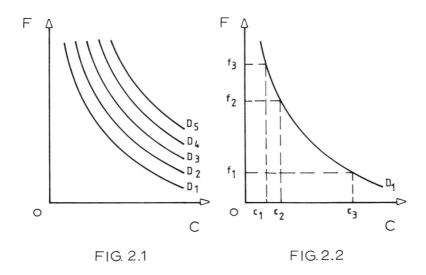

FIG. 2.1   FIG. 2.2

making up the indifference map. Along any single indifference
curve (for example D_1) in figure 2.2, Diana is indifferent between varying combinations of Food and Clothing: she has no
preference at all regarding whether she should have $Of_1 + Oc_3$,
$Of_2 + Oc_2$ or $Of_3 + Oc_1$ as all these combinations give her the
same level of satisfaction. The ratio of the sacrifice of
f_1f_2 of Food for c_2c_3 of Clothing is measured by the slope of
the straight line connecting points a and b (figure 2.3a).
   If we consider infinitesimal changes in the combinations
of Food and Clothing (figure 2.3b), the rate of change can be
measured by the slope of the tangent to the indifference curve
at the point under consideration. This is termed the marginal
rate of substitution in consumption between Food and Clothing
($MRS^C_{F,C}$).
   Since the indifference curves are convex from below, the
$MRS^C_{F,C}$ falls as one moves in either direction, indicating a
diminishing rate of substitution: as Diana gets more and more
Food (Clothing) she is less and less willing to take more and
more of it in exchange for Clothing (Food).
   Diana, like all other consumers, is assumed to prefer
more to less of both Food and Clothing; that is to say, all
commodities are 'goods' - none are 'bads' or 'neuters'. Hence
combinations given by indifference curve D_2 (figure 2.1) will
be preferred to combinations given by D_1, since one can always
find a point along D_2 which lies to the NE of a point on D_1.

11

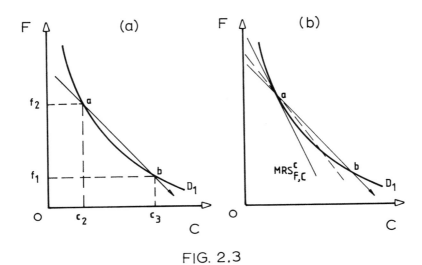

FIG. 2.3

For example, in figure 2.4, Z_2 is preferred to Z_1 since it offers more of both Food and Clothing. Z_3 is on the same level of satisfaction as Z_2 (Diana is indifferent between Z_2 and Z_3), hence although Z_3 offers less Food (but more Clothing) than Z_1, it will still be preferred to Z_1. It follows that combinations depicted by D_3 (figure 2.1) will be preferred to those depicted by D_2, combinations depicted by D_4 will be preferred to those given by D_3, etc. Hence Diana's indifference map depicts her consumption preferences: it shows combinations of Food and Clothing to which she is indifferent (those given along a single indifference curve), others she prefers (those combinations on indifference curves to the NE) and some she considers inferior to other combinations (those on indifference curves to the SW).

It should be noted that Diana's indifference curves do not intersect, otherwise we would have a contradiction in terms. This can be explained in the following way. Suppose they do intersect (figure 2.5): then Z_1 is inferior to Z_2 since Z_2 lies to the NE; Z_1 is on the same indifference curve as Z_4 therefore giving the same level of satisfaction as Z_4; Z_4 is preferred to Z_3 (as it lies to the NE) but Z_3 gives the same level of satisfaction as Z_2. In short, it is no longer possible to say that indifference curve D_1 is superior or inferior to indifference curve D_2. This possibility is ruled out by assuming that the consumer is rational and that commodities are goods. Going hand in hand with the assumption of

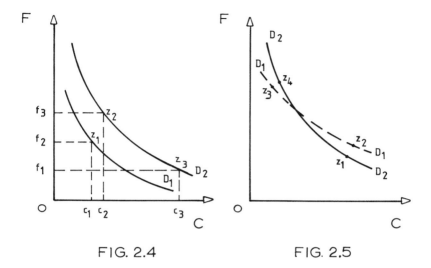

FIG. 2.4   FIG. 2.5

rationality is the notion of transitivity: if Diana prefers combination Z_2, say, to combination Z_1 and combination Z_3 to combination Z_2 then we assume that she prefers the combination given by Z_3 to that given by Z_1.

So let me summarise the characteristics of a consumer's indifference curves:

1. they slope downwards from left to right;
2. they are convex from below indicating a diminishing marginal rate of substitution in consumption;
3. they do not intersect; and
4. the further to the north-east a curve lies on the indifference map, the greater is the consumer's satisfaction.

1. Choice with expenditure constraint.

As consumers' financial resources are not infinite, almost everyone has constraints on their level of expenditure. For Diana, this constraint is given by her income; more precisely by that part of her income she plans to spend on Food and Clothing - the difference is due to her wish to save some of her income or to her plans to borrow and live beyond her means during the period under consideration. Hence: assuming that savings (S) and borrowing (B) do not depend on prices, i.e. they are exogenous (determined outside the system), Diana's

13

expenditure (E) can be stated as:
$$E = Y - S + B$$
where Y is her income. If we assume that Diana has a given
total expenditure for any given period of time and that the
prices of a unit of Food and Clothing are also given, then we
can show Diana's total possible purchases of Food and Clothing
by an expenditure line (figure 2.6). This shows that, given
the price of a unit of Food, if Diana decides to allocate her
total expenditure on Food alone, the maximum quantity she can
buy is OF. Similarly, if she decides to purchase Clothing
only the maximum she can buy is OC. It also follows that Diana
can purchase the different combinations of Food and Clothing
given along the straight line joining F and C.

Expenditure lines to the right of FC and parallel to it
indicate higher levels of expenditure given the same set of
prices and ones to the left of FC and parallel to it indicate
the contrary. Moreover, if we return to FC and assume a fall
in the price of a unit of Clothing while the price of a unit
of Food remains constant, the expenditure line pivots to the
right (figure 2.6b) to FC^2. And in the case of a rise in the
price of a unit of Clothing, it pivots to the left to FC^1.
The same also applies if the price of a unit of Food is changed
with the price of Clothing remaining constant: the expenditure
line FC pivots round C - see dotted lines around C. Finally,
it should be stressed that the slope of the expenditure line
measures the relative prices of Food (P_F) and Clothing (P_C):
P_C/P_F.

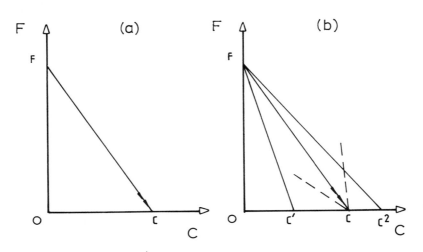

FIG. 2.6

In order to determine how much Food and Clothing Diana will actually purchase, we superimpose her expenditure constraint on her indifference map; assuming that she aims to maximise her satisfaction (remember Food and Clothing are goods) she will opt for the highest attainable combination. From figure 2.7 it can be seen that Diana can buy Z_1, Z_2, Z_3, or Z_4 but she cannot buy Z_5 since her expenditure is not high enough. If she buys Z_4 she will be underspending, so Z_4 is ruled out by assumption. The question is: which of Z_1, Z_2, Z_3 will Diana choose? The answer is simple: since Z_1 and Z_3 lie on the same indifference curve they give Diana the same level of satisfaction; but for the same expenditure she can buy Z_2, which gives her the highest possible level of satisfaction she can achieve. Note the characteristics of point Z_2: here the relative prices of Food and Clothing as measured by the slope of the expenditure line FC are exactly equal to the marginal rate of substitution in consumption between Food and Clothing ($MRS^C_{F,C}$) since FC is the tangent at that point. Hence the condition for optimisation is that: $MRS^C_{F,C} = P_C/P_F$. No other points on the expenditure line satisfy this condition.

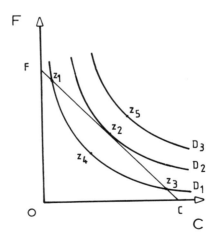

FIG. 2.7

2. The community.

From the consumption preferences for individual consumers we can now turn to those for the community as a whole and ask: is it possible to construct a community indifference map?

First, consider a community of two consumers: Diana and Mark. Diana's optimisation decision has already been discussed. Mark's can be determined in precisely the same manner, the only difference being that Mark's indifference map will not be the same as Diana's (unless of course they have precisely the same tastes). In an ideal market situation, Diana and Mark are faced with the same relative prices, i.e. it is assumed that sellers will not practise price discrimination between them. Hence optimisation is achieved as before for both Diana and Mark (figure 2.8), where FC and F*C* are parallel. For simplicity, the diagram is drawn on the assumption that the indifference curves for Diana and Mark are independent of each other. Diana and Mark are shown with <u>different</u> incomes: Diana has more to spend and that is why $\overline{OF} > \overline{O*F*}$ and $OC > O*C*$. Note that asterisks are used to distinguish Mark from Diana.

The question now is: can a single indifference curve for both Diana and Mark be constructed? Consider figure 2.8 carefully. Given their total expenditure, the prices of a unit of Food and Clothing and their consumption preferences, one knows that Diana will choose Of_1 of Food plus Oc_1 of Clothing and

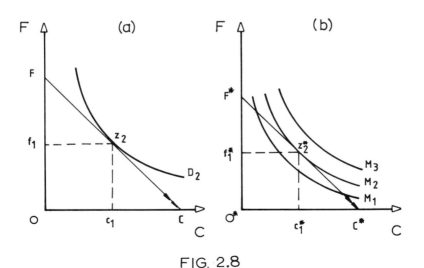

FIG. 2.8

Mark $O^*f_1^*$ plus $O^*c_1^*$. Hence the two together will choose $Of_1 + O^*f_1^*$ of Food in addition to $Oc_1 + O^*c_1^*$ of Clothing. This can be shown more conveniently by combining the two sections of figure 2.8 to make figure 2.9. The point O^* in relation to O shows the total of the two commodities that Diana and Mark will choose, given their expenditures and the prices of units of Food and Clothing. One is, therefore, able to say that the point O^*, which lies on a line parallel to FC, represents a joint point for both Diana and Mark equivalent to Z_2 and Z_2^* in the individual diagrams (figure 2.8): at O^* together they plan to consume Om of Food (equal to $Of_1 + O^*f_1^*$) and On of Clothing (equal to $Oc_1 + O^*c_1^*$). The particular advantage of this method is that a point of tangency of the two indifference curves simultaneously satisfies the optimisation condition for both Diana and Mark:

    (a) $MRS_{F,C}^c = (P_C/P_F)$ for Diana;

    (b) $MRS_{F,C}^c = (P_C/P_F)^*$ for Mark;

    (c)   also $(P_C/P_F) = (P_C/P_F)^*$, hence indicating perfect markets without price discrimination.

Now keep Diana's axes as they are and move the origin of Mark's axes around but in such a manner that the two indifference curves (D_2 and M_2) always remain at a tangent to each other (figure 2.10). For every point of tangency of D_2 and M_2 there is an equivalent O^* point. Each O^* point gives certain lengths of the Food and Clothing distances indicating a

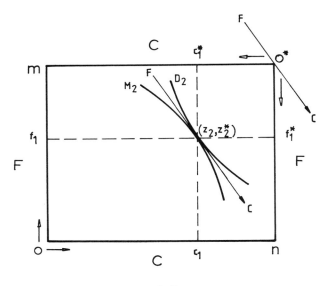

FIG. 2.9

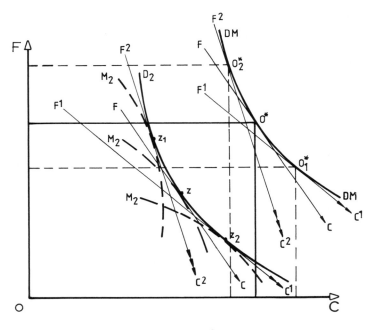

FIG. 2.10

particular level of total expenditure by Diana and Mark and a given relative price level. Therefore points like O^*, O_1^*, O_2^*, etc. show their total consumption at varying prices and at varying levels of expenditure. Hence, if the O^* origin is ignored, the smooth locus connecting all such points is an in-difference curve for <u>both</u> Diana and Mark. This operation can be repeated at higher or lower levels of indifference for both Diana and Mark by taking Diana's D_3 and Mark's M_3 and then repeating the process or by taking Diana's D_1 and Mark's M_1 and repeating the process. It can therefore be seen that an indifference map for both Diana and Mark, with similar char-acteristics to that of the individual consumer, can in fact be constructed (figure 2.11).

One can then introduce Frances. Take the combined indifference curve for Diana and Mark and repeat the process by
adding Frances's in the same fashion as Mark's was added to
Diana's. Then introduce Joan, Frank, Susan, David, Pamela,
Brenda, Kieran, Anthony, etc., until every single member of
the society is included.

3.   Caution.

There is, however, one problem which can be explained in the
following way. Return to figure 2.10 where the initial point
for Diana and Mark was Z, and assume, for the given Food and
Clothing distances indicated by O*, a different distribution
of the total of Food and Clothing between Diana and Mark. The
initial situation is given at Z in figure 2.12. Then at Z',
Diana is on a higher while Mark is on a lower indifference
curve but the total amount of Food and Clothing is exactly the
same as initially: Om of Food plus On of Clothing. Hence O*
is the same distance from O as before but it now lies on a
different slope since the slope of the common tangent at Z'
will not be the same as that at Z unless the indifference
curves have a particular shape: more precisely, unless they
are homothetic or exhibit characteristics of linear homogeneity of degree one – see below. If the common indifference
curve is then traced using the same procedure as before, it

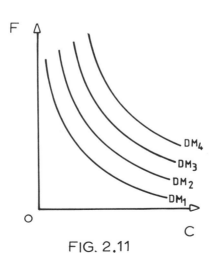

FIG. 2.11

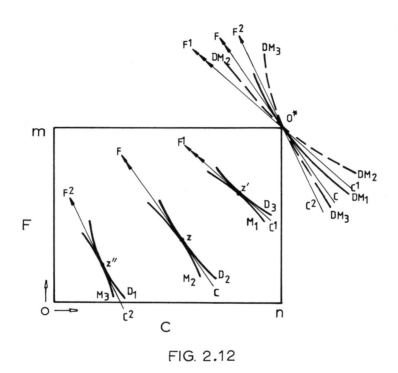

FIG. 2.12

will be found that the new indifference curve intersects the
old one: the new DM curve has to be at a tangent to F^1C^1.
This process can then be repeated at different levels of distribution: take point Z'' which takes Diana to a lower and Mark
to a higher indifference curve. Another common indifference
curve can then be traced at O^* which will be at a tangent to a
line parallel to F^2F^2 going through O^*. The result is that
community indifference curves (CICs) will intersect when distribution changes are introduced, making them different from
individual consumers' curves which, as explained earlier, can
never intersect.

The problem raised by intersection is that comparisons

become somewhat difficult: it is no longer possible to categorically state that one situation is better or worse than
another if the distributional weights in the two situations
are different. Note that this does not mean that no comparison can ever be made; this criticism is not valid when the distributional weight is unchanged. In order to avoid the distributional complication altogether it is possible to make one
of several assumptions:

    1. a community of identical citizens;
    2. a benevolent dictatorship;
    3. constant distributional weights;
    4. homothetic indifference curves, or ones exhibiting
characteristics of linear homogeneity of degree one. As mentioned earlier these are indifference curves of a particular
shape; more specifically they lie on the diagonal OO* with
expenditure lines (points of common tangency) parallel to each
other - thus only one community indifference curve can be generated (figure 2.13). In short, one can introduce assumptions
which rule out intersection. The assumption actually adopted
will depend on the use to be made of the CICs. It should be
stressed that whichever assumption is chosen certain comparisons will be ruled out but obviously the whole concept of
community indifference is not thereby rendered irrelevant.

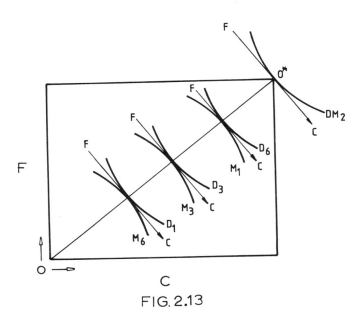

FIG. 2.13

Revealed Preference

The hypothesis of revealed preference analyses consumer behaviour in terms of the consumer's <u>actual</u> choice: the consumer
reveals his or her preference by choosing a particular combination of goods. It is therefore an ordinalist behaviourist
hypothesis which frees consumer analysis of the need for the
notion of indifference.
    Let us briefly recall the basic characteristics of this
hypothesis. The consumer, Diana, is assumed to be <u>rational</u>
in the sense that she prefers more to less, since commodities
are goods, none are bads or neuters. Diana's actual choice is
assumed to be <u>consistent</u>: if in a particular situation she is
observed to choose a certain combination of Food and Clothing,
she would opt for the same combination when faced with the
same choice again. Diana's choice is also supposed to be
<u>transitive</u>: if she prefers Z_1 to Z and Z_2 to Z_1, then she is
assumed to prefer Z_2 to Z.
    Diana has an expenditure constraint (budget restraint) and
faces given prices for a unit of Food and Clothing: P_C/P_F.
Suppose the budget restraint is FC (figure 2.14) and that
Diana is observed to choose the combination indicated by point
Z. This combination is therefore preferred to any other combination available to her (or is at least as good as any other
combination - see Michaely 1977, p.6). A rational consumer
will opt for combinations along FC, not ones inside the shaded
area.
    Suppose P_C falls (with P_F unchanged) while Diana's total
expenditure remains constant. The relevant budget line becomes FC' (figure 2.15). Diana will be acting perfectly rat-
ionally if she chooses any point along FC' except for F which
was rejected in the initial situation (the exception does not
apply when 'preference' and 'as good as' are considered to be
equivalent). Not only is Diana's choice a rational one but we
can also say that she is better off since the new choice available to her includes combinations which offer more of both
commodities.
    Now if we take away from Diana a Slutsky income-compensa-
tion (give her just enough to purchase Z when faced with the
new relative prices), the budget restraint will be F_1C_1
(parallel to FC'). It will be perfectly rational for Diana to
choose point Z or any point along ZC_1 since these combinations
were not available to her in the initial situation - note these
combinations offer her more Clothing and less Food. However,
we cannot say that any combination chosen along ZC_1 will make
her better off since her choice does not include any combination which gives her more of both commodities. It follows,
therefore, that any point chosen along a budget restraint which
crosses FC above Z can be described as leaving Diana better off
and any choice along a budget restraint which crosses FC below
Z cannot be ranked on a priori grounds alone. Also any budget

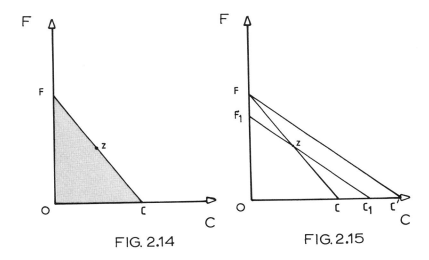

FIG. 2.14   FIG. 2.15

restraint which lies entirely to the right of FC is superior
to FC.
 We can apply these notions to the whole community.
Suppose the community was at point Z along F_1C_1 (figure 2.15)
in an autarkic situation (in a 'closed' economy) and selects
a point along FC made possible in an 'open' economy. Since FC
includes combinations which offer the community more of both
Food and Clothing we know the community must be better off.
However, we cannot infer from this that every single individual
is better off since the distribution of Food and Clothing in
the 'open' economy may be different from that in autarky: not
every individual will necessarily get more of both commodities.

The Analysis of Demand in International Trade

In such circumstances the hypothesis postulates that the 'open' economy situation is <u>potentially</u> better since those who gain overall can theoretically compensate those who lose and still be better off - here the usual 'compensation principles' apply. This argument does not apply in a situation in which FC is compared with relative prices which cut this line below Z; here no ranking is possible.

Conclusion

Some authorities have claimed (Michaely 1977, p. 5) that the hypothesis of revealed preference is superior to indifference analysis since it reaches the same conclusions on fewer assumptions (Occam's rule) and is adaptable to the community without additional assumptions. Moreover, Michaely also claims that the 'use of community indifference curves has long been known and recognized to be faulty' (p.4).

It should be apparent that Michaely's claim is unwarranted. Firstly, to postulate that the consumer's actual choice reflects rationality in a situation where all commodities are 'goods' implicitly assumes that the consumer must have some notion of indifference-preference: hence, in not facing up to this problem, the hypothesis of revealed preference is simply dodging the issue. Secondly, the notion that a certain combination of commodities is 'as good as' any other is wrong since it either suggests that the consumer's choice is purely arbitrary or that the consumer is unable to exercise choice - both are untenable since no <u>theoretical</u> construct can be built on such notions. Thirdly, and most importantly the revealed preference hypothesis cannot determine international prices since they have to be exogenously determined for the community to be able to make decisions; since it is the combined forces of supply and demand which determine prices, a hypothesis which cannot explain international prices is devoid of any <u>theoretical</u> significance. Finally, because of this, Occam's rule does not really apply here since like is not being compared with like.

Since the conclusions reached by adopting either approach are the same and since indifference analysis provides us with tools useful for representing international demand (see chapter 5), we shall adopt CICs in this book on the understanding that the problems they raise will be stressed and their implications explained as and when they arise.

Chapter Three

THE ANALYSIS OF SUPPLY IN INTERNATIONAL TRADE

Introduction

In chapter 2 a method was constructed for depicting the consumption preferences of the community as a whole, i.e. its
planned demand for Food and Clothing at various prices per
period of time given a certain set of market circumstances.
The purpose of this chapter is to devise a method for representing the total supply of Food and Clothing for the same
community.
    Basic economic theory includes the notion of a supply
curve representing the quantities of a commodity that producers plan to supply to the market at various prices in any
particular period of time given a certain set of market circumstances. In determining the planned supply of a commodity
it is important to consider the inputs that go into its production: their quantities and prices, the available technology
for combining them, etc. The relationship between factor inputs and the quantity of output can be represented by a 'production function' - PF. This can be illustrated using a two
dimensional diagram (figure 3.1): on the vertical axis we
measure the quantity of capital and on the horizontal the quantity of labour, i.e. number of man hours. The origin 0 is
that for Food. Then a PF for Food can be represented by a set
of isoquants, F_1, F_2, F_3, etc. An isoquant represents a given
level of output of the product under consideration (say F_1
means 20 units of Food) and this quantity can be produced by
various combinations of capital (K) and man hours (L): $k_1 + l_1$,
or $k_2 + l_2$ or $k_3 + l_3$, etc. can be used to produce F_1 or 20
units of Food. In short, one factor of production can be substituted for another. The slope of the isoquant gives, for
infinitesimal changes, the marginal rate of technical substitution in production $MRTS^P_{K,L}$ between K and L, i.e. the
$MRTS^P_{K,L}$ is measured by the slope of the tangent at the point
under consideration just as with the $MRS^C_{F,C}$ in the previous
chapter. The isoquants are convex from the origin indicating
a diminishing $MRTS^P$, i.e. as more K(L) is substituted for L(K),

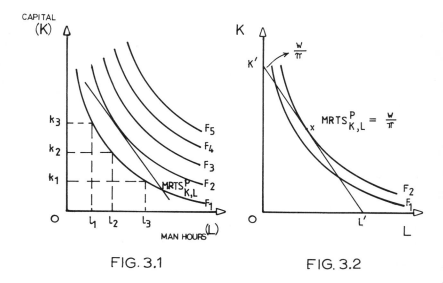

FIG. 3.1   FIG. 3.2

it becomes increasingly difficult to carry out further sub-
stitutions. Isoquants further away from the origin indicate
a higher level of output compared with ones nearer to the
origin. It must be stressed that it is the <u>complete map of
isoquants</u> which depicts the PF for a particular commodity.
    Each producer operates under different budget constraints
and given input prices. We will assume that the hiring price
of a unit of K (number of machine hours) can be expressed as π
(the rate of return on K) and the hiring price of a unit of L
(number of man-hours) as w (the wage rate). Producers are
assumed to aim for the most efficient input combination: in
other words they are profit maximisers or cost minimisers. The
budget can be represented in a similar way to the expenditure
line used in chapter 2: if the producer spends all his budget
on K alone, given π, the maximum he can hire is K' (figure 3.2).
Conversely, if he spends it all on L, given w, the maximum will
be L'. Hence the slope of K'L' measures the relative input
prices (w/π). Optimal choice is therefore determined by the
equality of the $MRTS_{K,L}^{P}$ and the relative input prices (w/π):
$$MRTS_{K,L}^{P} = w/\pi.$$
Hence at x we have the optimal combination of K and L given the
budget constraint – K'L' and the relative price ratio (w/π).
At x_1 the $MRTS_{K,L}^{P} > (w/\pi)$ and at x_2 the $MRTS_{K,L}^{P} < (w/\pi)$.
    It is possible to trace the paths generated by relative
changes in the factor prices (w and π) as well as the path generated by changing the size of the budget (figure 3.3). If

26

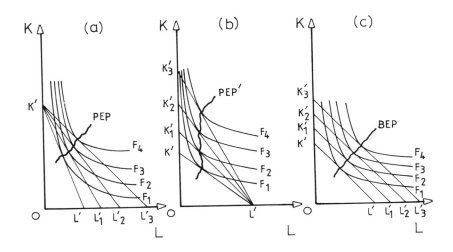

FIG. 3.3

w falls (with π remaining constant), the budget line pivots at K' in an anti-clockwise direction; if w increases, the budget line pivots in the opposite direction (figure 3.3a). Similarly, the budget line pivots at L' when π is changed with w being held constant - in the same way as the expenditure line in chapter 2 (see figure 3.3b). We can then trace all possible optimal points for a given budget and a fall in w with π held constant. In short we can produce higher levels of output for a given budget when the price of one factor falls with the other remaining constant. The resulting locus is called the price expansion path (PEP); similarly for a fall in π with w held constant, the PEP is PEP'. We can also hold w and π constant and trace the path generated by the optimal input combination as the size of the budget itself is altered; this is the budget expansion path, BEP (figure 3.3c).

Linear Homogeneous PFs

One of the PFs most widely used in economics is the LHPF (linear homogeneous PF of degree 1).
For a PF of the type:
$$Q = f \ (K, \ L, \ T)$$
we assume technology to be given; hence
$$Q = f \ (K, \ L).$$
An LHPF takes one of several specific forms: we shall use the

27

type which takes the form
$$Q = AK^{\alpha}L^{\beta}$$
where A is a constant and $\alpha + \beta = 1$.
The basic characteristics of this PF are:
(i)   If inputs are raised (lowered) by a certain percentage, output rises (falls) by the same percentage.
(ii)   The PF is differentiable:
$$dQ = (\partial Q/\partial K)\ dK + (\partial Q/\partial L)\ dL$$
where $\partial Q/\partial K$ and $\partial Q/\partial L$ are the marginal productivities of K and L respectively. Note that the marginal productivity of K(L) is the increase in Q due to using an extra unit of K(L) assuming that L(K) is constant. Also $\partial Q/\partial K = \pi$; $\partial Q/\partial L = w$.
(iii) For our purposes we assume that
$$\partial Q/\partial K\ ;\ \partial Q/\partial L > 0$$
i.e. if K $\uparrow$ $(\overline{L})$ Q$\uparrow$
     L $\uparrow$ $(\overline{K})$ Q$\uparrow$.
(iv)   We also assume that the second partial derivatives are negative; i.e. we assume the law of diminishing marginal productivity to be operative : as more and more L(K) is employed for a given quantity of K(L), the marginal productivity of L(K) declines:
$$\partial^2 Q/\partial K^2\ ;\ \partial^2 Q/\partial L^2 > 0.$$
(v)   In addition, we have mixed partial derivatives such that:
$$\partial^2 Q/\partial K\partial L\ ;\ \partial^2 Q/\partial L\partial K > 0.$$
That is, as the same quantity of L(K) works with more and more K(L), its marginal productivity increases.
(vi) As long as K and L are combined in the same proportion, their relative marginal productivities remain constant (but not equal). This means that the slopes of the tangents along any ray from the origin (i.e. at X_1, X_2, X_3) are equal - figure 3.4.
(vii) The distance along a ray from the origin measures the level of output such that distances twice as far from the origin along that ray indicate twice as much output.
    Before concluding this section there is a problem that should be discussed. Let us superimpose the sets of isoquants for Food and for Clothing (C_1, C_2, C_3, etc.) in the same K and L space and examine carefully what it would mean if these intersected more than once (see figure 3.5). Take C_1 and F_1. At points a and b the tangents to the isoquants are parallel to each other. These tangents measure both the $MRTS^P_{K,L}$ for the two commodities and the relative prices (w/π). The factor intensities (K,L) at a and b are measured by the slopes of the vectors from the origin : Oa and Ob. Since Oa is steeper than Ob, Clothing is K-intensive relative to Food. On the other hand, at a' and b', the vector Oa' is steeper than Ob', hence at relative factor prices (w/π)' Food is K-intensive relative to Clothing. This means that, if factor prices are widely different for the two industries in two different situations, (w/π) as against (w/π)', we can no longer categorically state

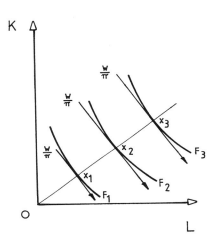

FIG. 3.4

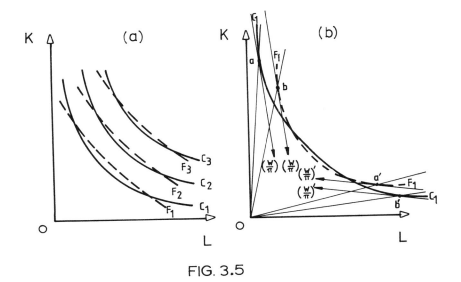

FIG. 3.5

The Analysis of Supply in International Trade

that Food or Clothing is either K-intensive or L-intensive throughout the analysis. This possibility is ruled out by the assumption that factor-intensity reversals do not occur with the result that the sets of isoquants for the two commodities do not intersect more than once: in figure 3.6 the vector Ob is steeper than Oa and the vector Ob' is steeper than Oa'. Hence Clothing is K-intensive relative to Food at all possible factor prices.

Edgeworth-Bowley Box Diagrams

The most convenient way of expressing how much of certain commodities a community is capable of producing given its total endowment of L and K and the use of the most efficient technological knowledge is by means of an Edgeworth-Bowley box diagram — figure 3.7. The advantage of the box is that it defines the total endowment of K and L: the total amount of capital available is $\overline{OK}$ and of labour $\overline{OL}$.

We can insert the LHPF for Food from origin O and for Clothing from origin O'. Some basic features now emerge: (i) If we are to ensure that the total endowment of K and L is always fully employed, then the output combination of Food and Clothing must be depicted by one point only. At x, the output of Food given by isoquant F_6 requires Ok_1 of K and Ol_1 of L; the output of Clothing given by C_3 requires $O'k*$ of K and $O'l*$ of L; hence the total quantity of K and L is exhausted. Note that if production of Food is given by x_3 and of

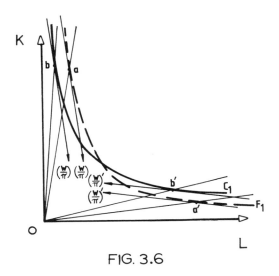

FIG. 3.6

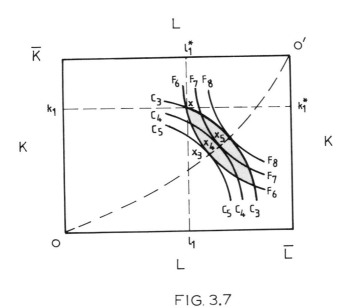

FIG. 3.7

Clothing by x_5, we have underemployment of K and L and it would be impossible to produce Food at x_5 and Clothing at x_3 since more K and L would be needed than is given by the size of the box.

(ii) To produce at x is inefficient since we could move to x_5 and have more Food with the same quantity of Clothing or move to x_3 and obtain more Clothing with the same quantity of Food. Also we can move to a point like x_4 and produce more of both commodities in comparison with x. In short, all points inside the shaded area are superior to x. Hence points such as x_3, x_4, x_5, which are more efficient than x, are determined by the tangency of the Food and Clothing isoquants, i.e. where

$$\text{MRTS}_{K,L}^{PC} = w/\pi = \text{MRTS}_{K,L}^{PF}.$$

This condition is satisfied only at the points of tangency since the slope of a common tangent measures both the $\text{MRTS}_{K,L}^{PC}$ and the $\text{MRTS}_{K,L}^{PF}$. It also follows that we can trace all points of common tangency between the Food and Clothing isoquants, this locus being a contract curve, points on which reflect efficient allocations of resources. However, we cannot rank points along the contract curve itself since to do so we need extra information: to distinguish between efficient points we need some 'outside' or exogenous valuation – we need a value judgement regarding the different allocations.

Also implicit in this is the assumption that factor inputs are not only homogeneous in nature but are also perfectly mobile between the two industries and that their prices are flexible. These assumptions ensure that 'factor markets' yield such efficient allocations which implies that producers are facing 'perfect' markets for K and L, i.e. the 'factor market' does not practise price discrimination between different productive agents.

(iii) Any point on the contract curve tells something about factor-intensities for the two industries. For example, at x_2 (figure 3.8), the ratio of K to L used in Food production, as measured by the slope of the vector OO_F, is less than that for the national average given by the slope of the diagonal OO'. At the same point, the K/L ratio for Clothing is higher than the national average, i.e. the vector $O'O_C$ is steeper than the diagonal. Hence Clothing is a K-intensive industry and Food is an L-intensive industry. The distances Ox_2 and $O'm_2$ measure the output of Food and Clothing respectively, while the slope of the tangent at x_2 measures the factor price ratio w/π as well as the relative marginal productivities of K and L. Hence at x_2, we know not only the output, but also the relative reward to K and L given in terms of Food and Clothing since the given number of man hours is multiplied by the wage rate per hour to determine the Wage Bill :

$$\text{Lxw} = \text{Wage Bill}$$

and the given quantity of K is multiplied by the rate of reward per unit (π) to determine the reward to K which, for simplicity, we shall call income from capital (YK):

$$\text{Kx}\pi = \text{YK}.$$

Now suppose this community decides to change the output-combination to x_4, i.e. it decides to produce more Food and less Clothing. As a result, the vectors measuring factor-intensities become steeper for both Food and Clothing: $O'O_C'$ is steeper than $O'O_C$ and OO_F' is steeper than OO_F. Hence both industries have become more K-intensive. This might seem like a contradiction in terms, particularly since the total quantities of K and L are constant. The explanation is quite simple: as K and L are released from Clothing, more K is made available than can be absorbed in the Food industry, given the initial factor prices. In order to ensure full employment of this

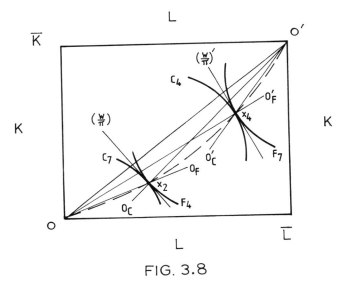

FIG. 3.8

extra K, an incentive has to be given to both industries to
make them employ it. One way of doing so is to lower the hiring price for a unit of K (π) relative to the hiring price of
a unit of man-hours – the wage rate (w) – which ensures that
both industries substitute K for L. Hence at x_4 the tangent
is steeper than at x_2. There is therefore no contradiction
because <u>overall</u> it is still true that Food is L-intensive and
Clothing is K-intensive in relation to the national average,
i.e. $O'O'_C$ is steeper than OO' (the diagonal) whilst OO'_F is
flatter than OO'. This result is ensured because the contract
curve lies consistently below the diagonal.

Note that if the contract curve lies consistently above
the diagonal, then Food will be the K-intensive industry and

Clothing the L-intensive one. Our conclusions are therefore basically still valid.

We have shown that a move from x_2 to x_4 produces a rise in w relative to π. Since K and L are constant, the result is that the wage bill (WB) rises relative to the reward to K (YK):

$$\frac{WB}{YK}\uparrow.$$

Hence the move from x_2 to x_4 favours L: income generated from these activities is redistributed in favour of L. The opposite result is achieved if it is decided to increase Clothing production and reduce Food production: in this situation both industries become more L-intensive and K is relatively better off, i.e.

$$\frac{WB}{YK}\downarrow.$$

It can therefore be seen that an Edgeworth-Bowley box diagram used in conjunction with the LHPFs provides valuable information. It should be stressed that understanding the box diagram and the information provided by it is particularly important for a proper understanding of later chapters.

Derivation of Production Possibility Frontiers

It was established above that the contract curve is the locus of the most efficient points of production. It was also stated that it is difficult to rank points along it since this requires certain preconceived ideas (i.e. exogenous factors) about the desirable income distribution implied by such a move. Let us now examine the contract curve in terms of Food and Clothing rather than of factor inputs (K and L).

We have already established that the distance of a vector from the relevant origin (0 or 0') measures the level of output of the commodity under consideration (Food or Clothing). Hence the distance 0a in figure 3.9 along the diagonal 00' is equal to F_2 units of Food; the distance 0a' is equivalent to F_4 units of Food; the distance 0a" is equivalent to F_6 units of Food, etc. Also the distances 0'b, 0'b', 0'b", etc. are equivalent to C_5, C_7 and C_9 units of Clothing respectively. Moreover, as we move along the diagonal we notice that a greater distance for one commodity is simultaneously accompanied by a shorter distance for the other: for example, if we start at b, we have C_5 units of Clothing and just less than F_6 units of Food; if we then move to a" we increase the output of Food to F_6 units and reduce the output of Clothing to just less than C_5 units. Hence we have situations where opportunity cost operates: it is not possible to have more of one product without having less of the other. The opportunity cost of having an extra unit of Food (Clothing) is the amount of Clothing (Food) sacrificed.

Now, let us use the corner $\overline{L}$ as the origin for the space measuring Food and Clothing (see figure 3.10). We can then

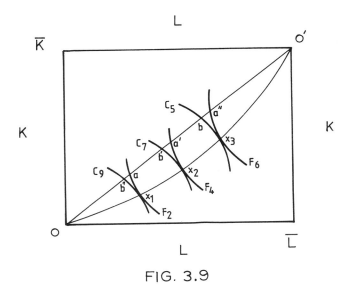

FIG. 3.9

take the information given by each point on the contract curve
and plot it in this commodity space. For example, at x_1 the
output of Food is measured along the diagonal by the distance
Oa, at x_2 by Oa', at x_4 by Oa'', etc. Because of the properties
of an LHPF of degree one, the relative lengths of these distances determine the relative output of Food. These distances
can, therefore, be plotted along the vertical axis of $\overline{L}$ to a_1,
a_2, a_3, etc., such that the ratio of $\overline{L}a_1$ to $\overline{L}a_2$ is equal to
the ratio of Oa to Oa', the ratio of $\overline{L}a_2$ to $\overline{L}a_3$ is equal to the
ratio of Oa' to Oa'', etc. In the same fashion the distances
$O'b$, $O'b'$, $O'b''$, etc. can be plotted along the horizontal axis
with $\overline{L}$ as the origin. Hence the distances $\overline{L}b_1$, $\overline{L}b_2$, $\overline{L}b_3$ are

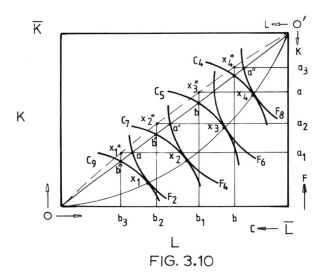

FIG. 3.10

related to O'b, O'b', O'b" respectively.

Having transferred the information given by the distances along the diagonal to the $\overline{L}$ space, we can now transfer the information given by the contract curve itself to this commodity space with $\overline{L}$ as the origin. Take point x_1 on the contract curve: at this point we know that the output of Food is given by a (i.e. $\overline{L}a_1$) and of Clothing by b" (i.e. $\overline{L}b_3$). Hence the total output of Food and Clothing at x_1 can be plotted on the commodity space as x_1^*. Then take x_2: here the outputs are given by a' and b' thus giving x_2^*. Hence, if we transfer the information given by all the points along the contract curve in this fashion we get the locus of these points as the curve

OO' which is concave from the origin $\overline{L}$. This new curve, which can now be detached from the box diagram (figure 3.11), is usually referred to as the Production Possibility Frontier (PPF) or the Production Possibility Curve (PPC) or the Transformation Curve. Note that its concavity from the origin is a reflection of increasing opportunity cost: whichever way one travels along the PPF the slope of the tangent becomes steeper. If opportunity cost reflects prices, the slope of the tangent at any point on the PPF reflects the relative prices of Food and Clothing, P_C/P_F.

Let us now digress and ask: could the PPF be a straight line and could it be convex from the origin? A straight line PPF would mean that the rate at which Food (Clothing) is sacrificed for Clothing (Food) would be constant through the whole scale of outputs, i.e. we would have constant opportunity costs with the relative price ratio P_C/P_F being constant irrespective of the production combination. The necessary condition for this is that the points x_1^*, x_2^*, x_4^*, etc. in the box diagram must lie along the diagonal OO'. Given the way we transformed the contract curve into a PPF, this can happen only if the contract curve itself is the diagonal so that the points x_1, x_1^*; x_2, x_2^*; x_4, x_4^*; etc. coincide (figure 3.12). Now if the PPF were the diagonal then the factor-intensities for Food and Clothing would be equal to each other and both would be equal to the national average (NA):

$$(K/L)^F = (K/L)^C = (K/L)^{NA}.$$

This implies that the two commodities are technically identical

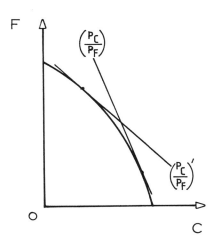

FIG. 3.11

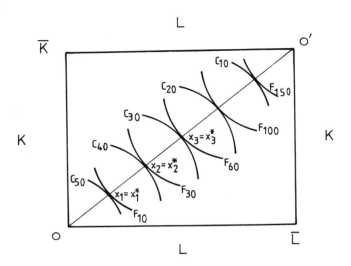

FIG. 3.12

which, in a two factor world, is a very restrictive assumption. The situation can arise only in the 'classical' world of a single factor of production, i.e. one has to assume a Labour Theory of value. Therefore, only under very restrictive assumptions can the PPF be a straight line. A PPF convex from the origin is possible and implies decreasing opportunity costs; the necessary condition for this is the existence of economies of scale – the level of output given by the set of isoquants is no longer consistent with that of a LHPF of degree one (figure 3.12). The assumption actually made about the shape of the PPF will depend on the use to which the concept is to be put.

   Let us now return to the PPF which is concave from the origin. We have established that every point on the PPF is equivalent to a point on the contract curve; that every point on the contract curve is a point of common tangency of the Food and Clothing isoquants and therefore determines a particular factor price ratio (w/π); and also that the tangent to any point on the PPF determines a particular level of opportunity cost or commodity price ratio P_C/P_F. Since every point on the contract curve determines an equivalent point on the PPF, the determination of the output combination automatically determines the equivalent factor prices: for every P_C/P_F there is a unique (w/π) ratio. Hence the beauty of this diagram is that it shows that factor prices are jointly and uniquely determined by the level of output.

Conclusion

The PPF represents the total planned supply of Food and Clothing per period of time at various prices given a certain set of 'market circumstances' in the society under consideration. It is therefore a simple and convenient way by which one can represent the total supply of these commodities for a community as a whole.

Chapter Four

GENERAL EQUILIBRIUM AND THE GAINS FROM TRADING

Chapter 2 demonstrated how the consumption preferences or planned demand for two broad categories of commodities (Food and Clothing) for the whole of a society can be represented on a community indifference map. In chapter 3 the total supply of these two commodities for the same society was depicted by means of a production possibility frontier - PPF. Since practically everything in economics is determined by supply and demand forces, it is now possible to use these two concepts to determine how a society reaches an optimum situation.

The Autarkic Society

Given the explicit assumptions that consumers are satisfaction maximisers and producers profit maximisers, what is the best combination of Food and Clothing this society can produce in an autarkic situation, i.e. without being exposed to international trade?

We know that the maximum amounts of Food and Clothing a society is capable of producing are given by its PPF (figure 3.11); points outside are not attainable whilst points inside indicate underemployment of resources, inefficient use of technology, or a combination of the two. We also know that the aim of a society is to reach the highest possible curve from its map of community indifference curves, CICs. If the PPF (HH) is superimposed on the map of CICs (figure 4.1), it can be seen that it is impossible for this society to attain CIC_4 (or higher CICs) since it lies outside its PPF. In an autarkic situation the society must satisfy its demand by its own supply: CIC_1, CIC_2, and CIC_3 are all attainable. It is apparent that point x gives the best production combination since it takes the society to the highest attainable CIC.

Point x has important characteristics. Firstly, the slope of the tangent at x measures the marginal rate of technical substitution in the production of Food and Clothing ($MRTS^p_{F,C}$), i.e. it measures the relative opportunity cost of Food and Clothing. Secondly, the slope of the tangent also measures the

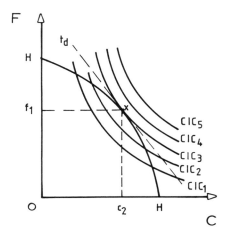

FIG. 4.1

marginal rate of substitution in consumption between Food and Clothing ($MRS^C_{F,C}$). Thirdly, the slope of the tangent is a reflection of the rate at which the society is willing to exchange the two commodities, i.e. it measures the relative prices of Food and Clothing (P_C/P_F) which are depicted by t_d, the domestic terms of trade for the home country, H. Point x is unique in that here all these conditions are equal; no other point along the PPF satisfies these conditions. At x:

$$MRTS^P_{F,C} = MRS^C_{F,C} = P_C/P_F = t_d.$$

The best production combination is therefore that indicated by point x, giving Of_1 of Food and Oc_2 of Clothing. In an autarkic society this production combination is the amount that will be consumed since domestic production is all that the society can consume.

The condition:

$$MRTS^P_{F,C} = MRS^C_{F,C} = P_C/P_F = t_d$$

is known as the Pareto-optimality condition which defines efficiency in the allocation of resources between the two sectors producing the commodities. As was seen in chapter 3, once the relative commodity prices (P_C/P_F) have been defined, factor prices (w/π) are automatically determined, and since the total quantity of capital and labour is given, the wage bill relative to the income from capital (WB/YK) is also determined, i.e. the relative income distribution between capital and labour has been established. Pareto-optimality does not specify whether this distribution is equitable; Pareto optimality is about efficiency not equity.

The Open Economy

Starting from the final position reached for the 'closed' - autarkic - economy (figure 4.1) one can ask: what incentive do producers and consumers need in order to become involved in international exchange? At this stage, the only sensible answer is that the international prices of Food and Clothing must be different from the relative prices in the 'closed' economy. If the international price is lower than the domestic price, the society as consumers will be happy to purchase from abroad but, since the society as producers cannot compete with cheaper imports, the production rate will be affected. Also if the international price is higher than the domestic price, the society as producers will be delighted to sell abroad and increase the domestic production rate; at the same time, the society as consumers will be happy to cut the consumption rate of this particular product. These considerations need careful examination. It must be pointed out immediately, however, that an implicit assumption has actually been made: by separating international prices from domestic - autarkic - prices it is implicitly assumed that the country does not play an active role in determining international prices. This can only be so if the country is so small that it does not exert any significant influence on the forces of supply and demand at the international level. This assumption is for simplicity, but in chapter 5 it will be removed and the implications examined.

Starting from an autarkic position and assuming that the country is suddenly (overnight) opened up for free international trade, the immediate effect (ignoring transport costs and any impediments on trade) is a change in the relative prices facing the society from t_d to t_i in figure 4.2. Production plans cannot be affected immediately, hence the initial result is that output will continue at x giving Of_1 of Food and Oc_2 of Clothing but the new relative prices (indicated by t_i) will move the consumption point from x to C_i' requiring Of_2 of Food and Oc_1 of Clothing. Since the need for Food is f_1f_2 more than initially, the country acquires that amount from abroad, i.e. the country needs to import f_1f_2. The excess supply of Clothing, c_1c_2, can be exported in exchange for the imports of Food at the international prices, i.e. $C_i'A/Ax$ is equal to the slope of t_i which represents the relative international prices.

A few interesting observations can be made with regard to the move from x to C_i'. Firstly, C_i' lies on a higher CIC (CIC_4): the society has therefore become better off, even though its production pattern is not disturbed. Secondly, at C_i' equality of $MRS_{F,C}^C$ and t_i is achieved. Thirdly, at x the

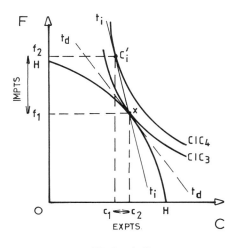

FIG. 4.2

$MRTS_{F,C}^{P}$ is no longer equal to t_i; indeed t_i is steeper than t_d at that point which means that Paretian optimality has been disturbed: $MRS_{F,C}^{C} = t_i > MRTS_{F,C}^{P}$. It is important to note that this consumption gain is valid in absolute terms since there is no change in the production combination (the country is still producing $Of_1 + Oc_2$) and therefore income distribution is unchanged; hence the set of CICs remains valid as before. This is called the <u>gains from exchange</u>.

The fact that the slope of t_i is steeper than that of t_d indicates that Food is relatively cheaper than Clothing in the international market, or alternatively that Clothing is relatively more expensive than Food in the domestic market. This means that producers have an incentive to produce for the international market and is also the reason why consumers decide to buy more Food and less Clothing, given t_i. In short, producers, who are assumed to be profit maximisers, will now expand their production of Clothing (since its relative price has risen) and contract their production of Food (since its relative price has fallen) – figure 4.3. Production will be expanded until t_i is just sufficient to cover the increasing opportunity cost of Clothing in terms of Food. Note that this is a final position because at P_i:

$$MRTS_{F,C}^{P} = t_i$$

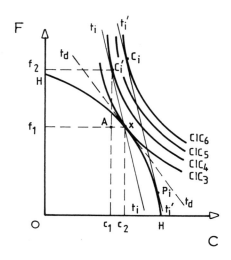

FIG. 4.3

and at C_i :
$$MRS_{F,C}^C = t_i.$$
Hence $\quad MRTS_{F,C}^P = MRS_{F,C}^C = t_i = (P_C/P_F).$

Note that $(P_C/P_F) = t_i$ because t_d and t_i are now equal. These, therefore, give Paretian optimality, but here defined to account for the 'open' economy, i.e. these are international Paretian conditions. Note also that exports and imports are determined by the right angled triangle determined by C_i and P_i.

General Equilibrium and the Gains from Trading

The Gains from Trade : Further Consideration

It has already been shown that the move from CIC3 to CIC4 (figure 4.3) is a pure gain due to international exchange. The move from CIC4 to CIC6 also reflects gains for the society as consumers, possible only because a decision is made to alter the initial production combination. Hence these new gains are entirely due to the society's increased specialisation in the production of Clothing at the expense of Food production; they are the gains from specialisation.

There are therefore two aspects to international trade: gains due to exchange and gains due to specialisation. It has been established that the gains from exchange are unequivocal since income distribution is not affected – one of the basic assumptions for deriving well-behaved CICs. The gains from specialisation are not so unequivocal.

The move from CIC4 to CIC6 is possible only because the production combination can be adjusted. However, in the construction of the PPF from the box diagram it became quite clear that any move along the contract curve entails a change in the distribution of the total amount of Food and Clothing and therefore a change in the relative rewards to capital and labour, i.e. WB/YK changes – see chapter 3. If distribution has changed (here in favour of capital since Clothing is capital-intensive), can it still be maintained that the gains from trading have been unequivocal? If income distribution changes, the original set of CICs is no longer valid, i.e. it is no longer possible to categorically state that one CIC gives a higher or lower level of satisfaction than another.

It is quite clear that the gains from exchange are unequivocal but the gains from specialisation raise certain problems. However, it can safely be stated that limited trade (that is, the international exchange of a given initial endowment of Food and Clothing) is better than no trade; in other words the gains from exchange still justify trading given the assumptions that have been made. Moreover, if any of the assumptions made at the end of chapter 2 (a society run by a benevolent dictator, a society of identical citizens, constant distributional weights, etc.) is adopted, the result is that the gains from specialisation, if no compensation is made to labour in this situation, are at least potential gains. Therefore, it can categorically be stated that free trade is potentially better than no trade and that limited trade is unequivocally better than no trade, given the assumptions that have been made.

The Home and Foreign Countries

The discussion so far has concentrated on one 'small' country. However, the argument can easily be extended to two countries: (i) Assume that the two countries have the same demand pattern but different PPFs so that CIC_2–CIC_7 apply to both and HH and WW are the PPFs for the home country (H) and the rest of the world (W) respectively – figure 4.4. Then in autarky, H is at x with a relative price ratio determined by the slope of the tangent of CIC_2 to HH. W is at x^* with its relative price ratio determined by the slope of the tangent of CIC_5 to WW. Assume an international relative price ratio of t_i which is somewhere between the two autarkic ratios. As a result H specialises more in the production of Food (P_i) and its equilibrium consumption becomes C_i while W specialises more in the production of Clothing (P_i^*) and its consumption point moves to C_i^*. Hence H needs to import C_iA and to export P_iA while W needs to import C_i^*B and export P_i^*B. These quantities can be exchanged at the international relative price ratio,

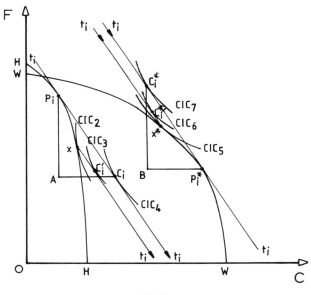

FIG. 4.4

General Equilibrium and the Gains from Trading

ti (the slopes of the t_is are equal indicating that H and W
are facing the same relative prices). Note that the distance
P_iA is equal to C_i^*B and the distance C_iA is equal to P_i^*B since
H's exports are W's imports and H's imports are W's exports.
For H the move from CIC_2 to CIC_3 shows the gains from exchange
and the move from CIC_3 to CIC_4 shows the gains from specialisation. For W the moves from CIC_5 to CIC_6 and from CIC_6
to CIC_7 give the equivalent gains. Hence both countries
gain from trading. Note that since t_i is different from the
domestic relative prices for both H and W it follows that it
is no longer assumed that either country is 'small'.
(ii) Similar results can be obtained assuming H and W have
different demand patterns but the same PPF (figure 4.5) and

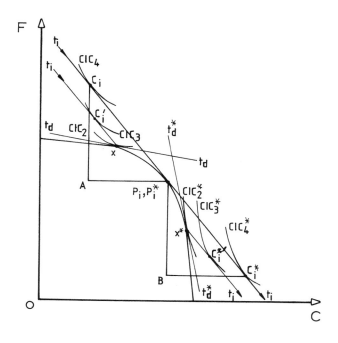

FIG. 4.5

also assuming they have different demand patterns as well as different PPFs (figure 4.6)

Note, however, that t_i has so far been arbitrarily determined. It is obvious that t_i must be objectively arrived at; this is discussed in the next chapter.

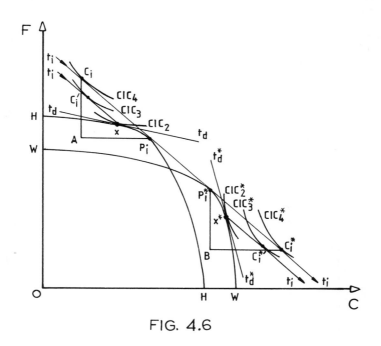

FIG. 4.6

Chapter Five

THE DETERMINATION OF THE TERMS OF TRADE

Introduction

The discussion of the gains from international trading in
chapter 4 was rather limited since it established only in an
arbitrary way how the international price ratio, t_i, is determined. It will be remembered that the country under consideration was assumed to be so small that its actions exerted
no influence on the international economy. However, when
countries are not small they play an active role in determining the international supply of and demand for traded goods.
It is then no longer justifiable to assume that t_i is given or
exogenously determined: t_i has to be determined inside the
system, or endogenously. The aim of this chapter is to show
how this is achieved.

First, however, it should be remembered that the international price ratio is usually referred to as the terms of
trade (t/t) which, in a highly simplistic analysis, can be defined as the ratio of the price of exports (P_X) and the price
of imports (P_M) such that:
$$t/t = P_X/P_M.$$
In a more realistic situation, P_X and P_M will reflect an index
of a large number of commodities, i.e. t/t will be a weighted
index of export and import prices. t/t is determined by
supply and demand forces just like any other price, but the
supply and demand forces in this case are specifically those
relating to the international market. Hence, t/t as a price
ratio is determined by the international supply of and demand
for internationally traded goods. International supply, it
will be remembered represents the excess domestic supply of a
commodity and international demand the excess domestic demand
for a commodity - see figure 5.1. 'Excess supply' and 'excess
demand' are usually expressed in terms of the amount a country
is prepared to offer as exports in exchange for what it needs
as imports. In order to derive offer curves (offer curves reflect the international supply of and demand for internationally traded goods), hence to determine t/t, it is necessary,

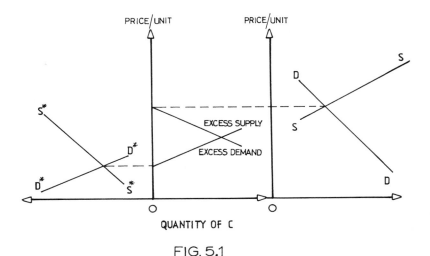

FIG. 5.1

as a starting point, to derive trade indifference curves (TICs).

Trade Indifference Curves

To construct TICs we must return to the Paretian Optimum for an autarkic economy established in chapter 4 - see figure 4.1 where our community produces and consumes Of_1 of Food and Oc_2 of Clothing, i.e. its consumption possibilities are confined to its PPF (HH). There is, therefore, no international trading. Put differently, at the relative domestic price ratio t_d, this country is not interested in international trading; it has no incentive for doing so since its domestic production is just sufficient to satisfy its domestic consumption at the given relative prices.

For simplicity, the diagram can be turned anticlockwise $90°$ to obtain the position depicted in figure 5.2. There is no particular novelty in this anticlockwise move except that the horizontal axis can now be extended to the right and the two new axes can be used in the usual fashion.

If Food and Clothing are to be considered as commodities that can be exported and imported, i.e. as exportables and importables, it can be stated that at a relative international price ratio t_i equal to t_d, giving exactly the same relative prices (P_C/P_F), H is not interested in international trade. Therefore, if the new axes (in the right hand quadrant)

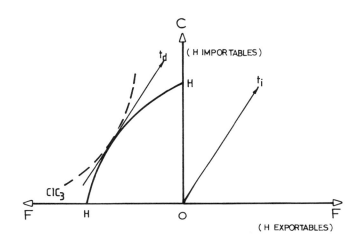

FIG. 5.2

measure exportables and importables, then at t_i H will be at O indicating a zero quantity of both Food and Clothing offered for international trading.

The PPF can be thought of as a block fixed to its own origin so that HOH and all the vectors from O to HH remain constant. HOH can then exist separately from the rest of the diagram. The significance of this is that certain manoeuvres are now possible which could not be performed otherwise: HOH can be plotted anywhere, leaving us free to use the original axes (those of the left hand quadrant) to depict the consumption preferences for H. Remembering that the CICs are fixed to the original axes, move HOH to the NE keeping it tangential to CIC_3 – figure 5.3. In the process, the origin of HOH traces a path known as a trade indifference curve for H (TIC_1).

It is important to explain the name TIC. The main origin, O, has already been decided upon as the origin for the right hand quadrant measuring Food and Clothing as exportables and importables. It has also been established that given t_i (i.e. a relative price ratio exactly equal to the autarkic ratio in H, t_d), H offers zero quantities of both Food and Clothing for trading internationally. Now, take HOH to the NE keeping it tangential to CIC_3. At x_3^*, for example, given the origin of HOH and t_i', H is prepared to produce Oc_1 of Clothing and Of_5 units of Food. However, given t_i', H plans to consume Of_3 of Food and Oc_5 of Clothing. This means that, given t_i', H plans

51

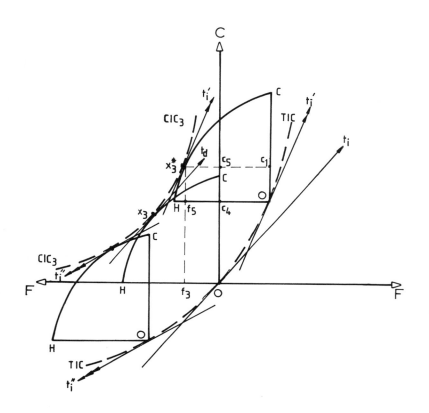

FIG. 5.3

to produce Oc_4 of Clothing short of its planned domestic demand (it plans to produce Oc_1, which is equal to c_4c_5, and plans to consume Oc_5 creating an excess demand for Clothing equal to c_4c_5. Also, given t_i', H will have an excess supply of Food equal to Oc_4 (read along the horizontal axis of HOH) since it plans to produce Of_5 and to consume Of_3 (which is equal to c_4f_5). The excess supply of Food, Oc_4, can be exported in exchange for imports of Clothing of Oc_4 which is the excess demand for Clothing, these two quantities being exchanged at t_i'. These exports and imports leave H on the same level of community satisfaction as in the autarkic situation, CIC_3. From the way TIC_1 has been traced it follows that this analysis can be repeated at every point along it. Hence each point on TIC_1 is equivalent to a particular point along CIC_3 and the equivalent points lie on equal slopes. It therefore follows that movements along TIC_1 trace different quantities that H is prepared to export in exchange for varying quantities of imports at various relative price levels. Note that if infinitessimal changes are being considered then the slope at any point along TIC_1 can be approximated by the slope of a vector from O to that point. These varying quantities of exports and imports leave H on the same level of community satisfaction, CIC_3. Hence H is indifferent between these varying levels of international trading: a Trade Indifference Curve.

The process can be repeated at different levels of community satisfaction. Take CIC_4, place HOH tangential to it at a particular point, e.g. x_4 – (figure 5.4) and trace TIC_2. Hence H needs to import Oc_5 of Clothing in exchange for Oc_5 (along the horizontal section of HOH) of Food given t_i'. This can be repeated for different points along TIC_2. Then again at still higher levels of community satisfaction: CIC_5, CIC_6, etc. to obtain a map of trade indifference curves – figure 5.5. Since each TIC is equivalent to a particular CIC and since moving in the NW direction along TICs is equivalent to moving to higher CICs, it is then established that H will be better off moving in this direction. Obviously, H will be worse off moving in the opposite direction.

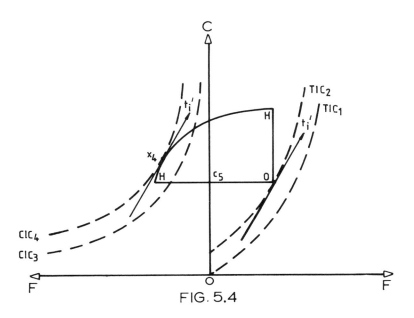

FIG. 5.4

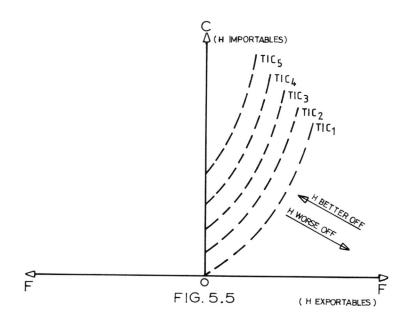

FIG. 5.5

At this stage it is necessary to discuss a few points so far omitted. Let us return to the starting point for the derivation of TICs. Here: (a) the TICs could have been extended to the W and SW of the NE quadrant and (b) one could also have started with a TIC to the SE of TIC_1 (TIC_0) – figure 5.6. The reasons for concentrating on the TICs in the NE quadrant beginning with TIC_1 are as follows. Firstly, extending the TICs to the SW quadrant would simply have generated two sets of TICs; those in the NE quadrant would indicate, as already explained, that Clothing makes up H's importables and Food its exportables, and those in the SW would simply reverse the pattern of trade with Clothing becoming the exportables and Food the importables. Since a single country cannot be in both states <u>simultaneously</u> it is necessary to concentrate on one only of the two quadrants, at least for the time being. Here the NE quadrant has been chosen. Secondly, take the sections of the TICs which lie in the NW quadrant. For example, if we plot HOH at a tangent to TIC_2, H plans to produce Oc_4 of Clothing and Of_2 of Food – read from HOH. It also plans to consume Oc_6 and Of_3 of Clothing and Food respectively. Hence, to be at X_4^*, H will have to be an importer of both Food and Clothing since it has an excess demand for both – f_3f_2 and c_4c_6 respectively. In a real international economy this can never be the case since a country must have exports to pay for its imports. (It can be true in very

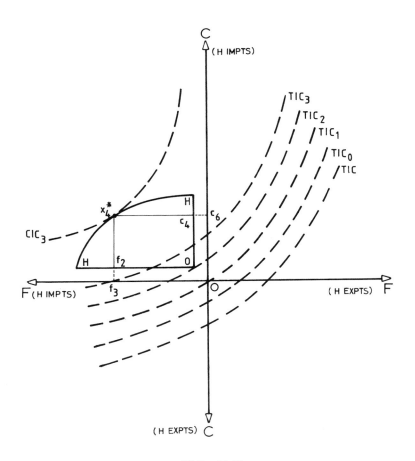

FIG. 5.6

special non-market situations and for a specified period of time, e.g. for a very poor country for which the international community assumes responsibility – see chapter 9.) Thirdly, if the TICs were to be extended to include those like TIC_0, this country would initially have to be at a CIC below the one it reached in autarky: H would have to be either an exporter of both Food and Clothing or an exporter of one without being an importer of the other, which can never be true in a two-country two-commodity world. The TICs therefore start with TIC_1 and are restricted to ones to the NW of it; all are within the NE quadrant and none touch the axes.

The Determination of the Terms of Trade

Trade Indifference Curves for the Rest of the World

The trade indifference curves for the foreign community, W,
can be derived in the same fashion. Start from the autarkic
position for W (figure 5.7a) but this time rotate clockwise
90° (figure 5.7b). It is then possible to continue to use the
NE quadrant for Food and Clothing as exportables and importables. Now visualise WOW as fixed to its own origin and repeat the process performed for H – figure 5.8a. Then consumption and production effects are the excess supply of Clothing
and the excess demand for Food, giving trade indicated by the
triangle Of_6O at the relative international price ratio t_i^2.

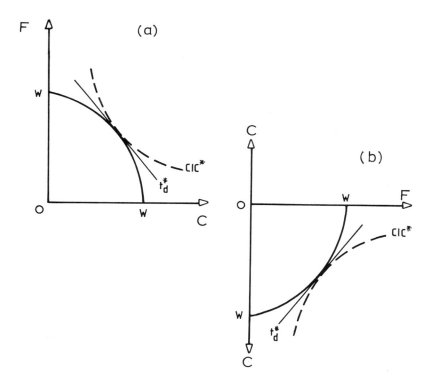

FIG. 5.7

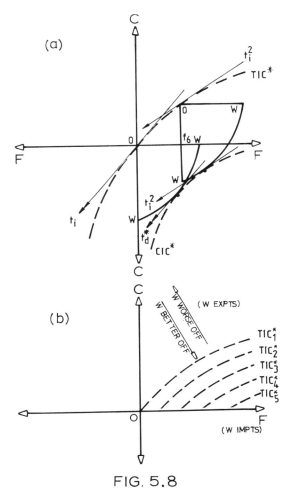

FIG. 5.8

This can be repeated for different levels of CIC*s to obtain the map of TIC*s given in figure 5.8b. It should be stressed that the TIC*s must be confined to the NE quadrant without touching the axes and beginning with TIC_1^* for similar reasons to those applied to the TICs. Hence the set of TICs for W shows that a move to the SE renders W better off and a move to the NW worse off.

The Home Country and the World

It is now possible to use the NE quadrant to superimpose the sets of TICs for both H and W – figure 5.9. Clothing makes up

57

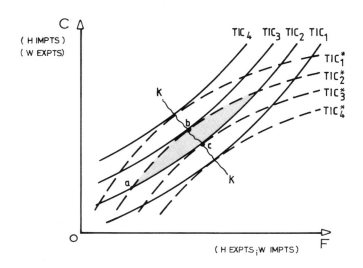

FIG. 5.9

H's importables and W's exportables while Food makes up H's
exportables and W's importables: one country's exports are
another country's imports.

Once the two sets of TICs are superimposed on the same
commodity space, two basic features emerge. Firstly, it is
now possible to state that a move in the NW direction not only
indicates an increase in the welfare of H but also simultaneously indicates a reduction in the welfare of W. The opposite
is also true: a move in the SE direction indicates an increase
in the welfare of W simultaneously with a deterioration in the
welfare of H. Secondly, since the sets of TICs slope differently (TICs are convex from below whilst TIC*s are concave
from below), a locus of common tangencies can now be traced.
This locus is a contract curve (KK) - see figure 5.9 - with
similar characteristics to those already encountered. Firstly,
any point on the contract curve is superior to a point outside
it - b and c are superior to a since they give a higher level
of satisfaction for one country with the other country remaining on the same level of satisfaction. Secondly, any point
inside the shaded area is superior to a. Thirdly, since all
points on the KK are efficient and since a movement along the
KK indicates that one country can be made better off only at
the expense of the other, points along the KK cannot be ranked
without introducing some extraneous factor, i.e. without introducing some exogenous valuation.

The Determination of the Terms of Trade

Constant Opportunity Costs

To conclude this section on TICs it is necessary to state
briefly what the shape of the TICs will be when there are
constant opportunity costs - decreasing opportunity costs are
discussed in chapter 14.
     Recall that when opportunity costs are constant the PPF
will be a straight line. Then for H a TIC will take the shape
shown in figure 5.10a. Repeating for higher CICs we get the
map of TICs shown in figure 5.10b. Note that the TICs have a
straight section and a section which is convex from below.
For W simply repeat the process to arrive at the map of TIC*s
given in figure 5.10c.
     By superimposing the TICs and TIC*s on the same commodity
space we get the contract curve KK shown in figure 5.10d.

Offer Curves

As we have seen, TICs on their own do not provide all the information needed to determine t/t (or t_i) since all they depict is _various_ levels of international trade a country is
prepared to engage in which result in different levels of community satisfaction. What we are really interested in is the
precise planned quantities of exports and imports of the
country under consideration. TICs can be used to extract this
precise information. The aim of this section is to do that.

Offer Curves for the Home Country

(a) Increasing opportunity costs.
     Recall that with increasing opportunity costs the PPF is
concave from the origin. This produces TICs for H of the
shape shown in figure 5.5.
     However, as already mentioned, TICs depict various levels
of international trading which correspond to different levels
of community satisfaction. What we need to know is the exact
planned quantities of exports and **imports.** These cannot really
be specified without some knowledge of the relative international prices of these commodities, i.e. (P_C/P_F), which can
readily be obtained in the manner hinted at in the previous
section: recall that we inserted vectors from the origin 0 to
the NE space, such as t_1^1, t_1^2, t_1^3, etc. (figure 5.11). The
slopes of these vectors measure the quantities of Food and
Clothing that can be exchanged for each other; hence they
measure (P_C/P_F). When the t_is rotate anticlockwise, the relative price of Food rises while that of Clothing falls: for
any given quantity of Food offered more Clothing can be obtained in exchange since the slopes of the t_is become steeper.
Alternatively, for any given quantity of Clothing, a clockwise
move indicates that increasing quantities of Food can be obtained in exchange for the given quantity of Clothing. In

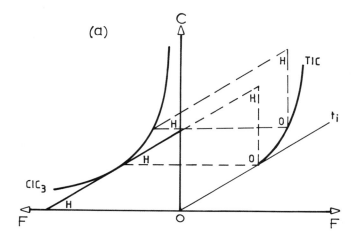

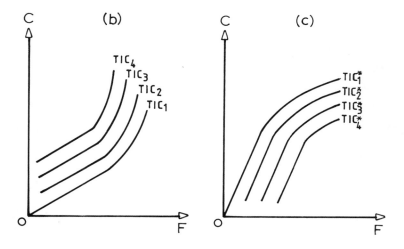

FIG. 5.10

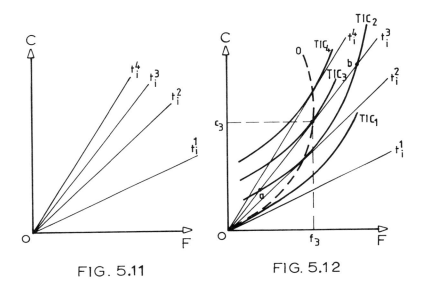

FIG. 5.11   FIG. 5.12

short, a clockwise rotation of t_i is favourable to Clothing since (P_C/P_F) rises and is simultaneously unfavourable for Food. An anticlockwise rotation has the opposite effect.

Now if a set of t_is, such as t_i^1, t_i^2, t_i^3, .., etc., is superimposed on the map of TICs (figure 5.12), it will be noticed that each TIC is tangential to a particular level of t/t; also that TIC_1 is tangential to t_i^1 at the origin. This is due to the fact that t_i^1 is equal to t_d, hence at these t/t H has no incentive for trading.

The extra information gained from the superimposition of the TICs and t_is on the same commodity space is that of depicting the exact planned quantities of exports and imports that H will plan to engage itself in at various t/t. For instance, when t/t is that given by t_i^3, H will plan to import Oc_3 in exchange for exports equal to Of_3 (figure 5.12). All other combinations such as those given by a and b will be rejected since they give a lower level of community satisfaction: recall that a move in the NW direction is equivalent to a higher level of community satisfaction for H. Levels of trading indicated by TIC_4, TIC_5, etc. are of course not feasible given t_i^3. This reasoning can be applied to different TICs and t_is.

Since there are a large number of TICs and since an equally large number of vectors can be drawn from the origin, it follows that there will be a large number of points where

each TIC is tangential to a t_i. We can trace all such points to get a locus (figure 5.12). This locus is called H's (trade) offer curve (OO) since it traces the precise quantities of exports H is prepared to exchange for precise quantities of imports given certain t/t. This is due to the way OO has been constructed: each point along it lies on a TIC which is tangential to a t_i.
(b) Constant opportunity costs.

When there are constant opportunity costs, the PPF, as we have seen, is a straight line, and the TICs have a portion which is a straight line and a portion which is concave looked at from the SE.

If a set of t_is is now superimposed on the map of TICs, and H's offer curve is traced as before (figure 5.13), it will be obvious that the straight line section of TIC_1 coincides with t_i^1 and that is the reason for the shape of the offer curve.

Offer Curves for the World

Following the above procedure we can also derive the offer curves for the world (OO*) for the two cases of increasing and constant opportunity costs.

In the case of increasing opportunity costs the TICs for the world will be concave from below and the offer curve will have the shape shown in figure 5.14a.

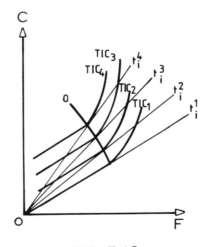

FIG. 5.13

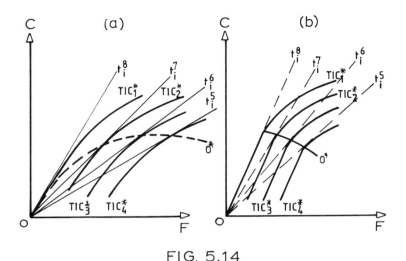

FIG. 5.14

With constant opportunity costs the TIC*s will have a straight line section and a section concave from below. Hence OO* will have the shape shown in figure 5.14b.

Elasticity of Offer Curves

Before concluding this section it is necessary to discuss the slope of the offer curve. Take the offer curve for H which is derived on the assumption of increasing opportunity costs (figure 5.12). Any point on OO depicts the quantity of Clothing imports (the vertical distance) H plans to purchase in exchange for a given planned quantity of Food exports (the horizontal distance). Such quantities have the same value since the vectors from the origin to such points represent the relative prices of Food and Clothing (P_C/P_F). Hence with each such t_i is associated a net planned demand for Clothing imports and equivalently valued net planned Food exports. Note that as Clothing becomes progressively cheaper (i.e. the vectors from the origin move in an anticlockwise direction), more quantities of Clothing imports are demanded, but H need not continue to offer larger amounts of Food exports in exchange. In other words, at one stage OO begins to bend backwards: up to point n (figure 5.15) the exchange of Food and Clothing requires increasing quantities of both; after point n more Clothing imports are demanded in exchange for smaller quantities of Food exports.

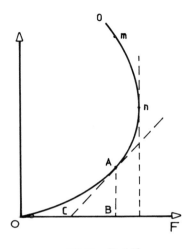

FIG. 5.15

The precise concept defining these considerations is the elasticity of the offer curve: the degree of responsiveness of Clothing (Food) to a small change in the quantity of Food (Clothing). More formally, the elasticity of the offer curve ε_0 is defined as:

$$\varepsilon_0 \equiv \frac{\% \text{ change in imports}}{\% \text{ change in exports}}$$

$$= \frac{dC/C}{dF/F}$$

$$= \frac{dC}{dF} \cdot \frac{F}{C} \cdot$$

For instance, at point A (figure 5.15) on H's offer curve, ε_0 is measured in the following way. Draw the tangent to OO at point A and let it intersect the horizontal axis at point C. Draw a vertical line through A and let it intersect the horizontal axis at point B. The slope of the tangent to OO at point A coincides with the derivative dC/dF at A. Therefore,

$$\varepsilon_0 = \frac{BA}{BC} \times \frac{OB}{BA}$$

$$= \frac{OB}{BC} \cdot$$

Note that as long as point C lies between the origin, O, and point B, the elasticity of the offer curve must be positive and greater than unity. If the offer curve is a straight line

64

point C will coincide with the origin and the elasticity of the offer curve will be equal to unity at all points on the offer curve. If the offer curve is backward bending then at any point, say m, point C will lie to the right of point B; the distance BC will be negative and so will the elasticity of the offer curve. This result is due to the fact that the derivative dC/dF at the backward bending portion of the offer curve is negative. At the point where the offer curve stops sloping upwards and begins bending backwards (i.e. at point n in figure 5.15 where the tangent to the offer curve is the perpendicular), the elasticity of the offer curve becomes infinite, since OB is strictly positive whilst BC becomes equal to zero.

Hence the offer curve exhibits elasticity of unity at the origin, becomes increasingly elastic up to the point at which the tangent to the offer curve is the perpendicular where the elasticity is infinite and finally becomes increasingly inelastic after that point along the backward bending part.

There are two other elasticity concepts that should be noted:
(a) The elasticity of demand for imports ε_M^D, defined as:

$$\varepsilon_M^D = \frac{\% \text{ change in imports}}{\% \text{ change in the relative price of imports}} \ .$$

Along the offer curve the value of imports equals that of exports ($P_C \times Q_C = P_F \times Q_F$). Hence the relative price of imports (P_C/P_F) is determined by Q_F/Q_C or F/C for simplicity. Then ε_M^D is equal to:

$$\varepsilon_M^D = \frac{dC/C}{d(F/C)/(F/C)} = \frac{dC}{d(F/C)} \ \frac{F}{C^2} = \frac{dC}{(CdF - FdC)/C^2} \ \frac{F}{C^2}$$

$$= \frac{(dC/dF)(F/C)}{1 - (dC/dF)(F/C)} = \frac{\varepsilon_0}{1-\varepsilon_0} \ . \tag{3}$$

Since ε_0 = OB/BC we can measure ε_M^D as :

$$\varepsilon_M^D = \frac{\varepsilon_0}{1-\varepsilon_0} = \frac{OB/BC}{1 - (OB/BC)} = \frac{OB}{BC - OB} \ . \tag{4}$$

Equation (3) can be expressed in terms of ε_0, hence

$$\varepsilon_0 = \frac{\varepsilon_M^D}{1+\varepsilon_M^D} \ . \tag{5}$$

ε_M^D is generally negative (since even if imports are a Giffen good, they are identical with domestic consumption minus domestic production; hence, even if domestic consumption falls as imports become cheaper, it does not necessarily follow that imports will also fall since domestic production also falls – imports will fall if, and only if, domestic consumption falls faster than domestic production). If ε_M^D exceeds unity in absolute terms ($\varepsilon_M^D < -1$), $\varepsilon_0 > 0$ and the offer curve will be upward sloping. However, if the demand for imports is inelastic ($-1 < \varepsilon_M^D < 0$), $\varepsilon_0 < 0$ and the offer curve will be backward bending.
(b) The elasticity of supply of exports, ε_X^S, defined as:

$$\varepsilon_X^S = \frac{\% \text{ change in exports}}{\% \text{ change in the relative price of exports}} \cdot \qquad (6)$$

Since the relative price of exports is equal to (P_F/P_C) it is given along the offer curve as C/F. Substituting C/F into (6) one gets:

$$\varepsilon_X^S = \frac{dF/F}{d(C/F)/(C/F)} = \frac{dF}{d(C/F)} \frac{C}{F^2}$$

$$= \frac{dF}{(FdC - CdF)/F^2} \frac{C}{F^2} = \frac{1}{(dC/dF)(F/C) - 1} = \frac{1}{\varepsilon_0 - 1} \qquad (7)$$

Since $\varepsilon_0 = \frac{OB}{BC}$ we can measure ε_X^S as:

$$\varepsilon_X^S = \frac{1}{\varepsilon_0 - 1} = \frac{1}{(OB/BC) - 1} = \frac{BC}{OB - BC} \cdot \qquad (8)$$

If we add ε_M^D and ε_X^S from equations (3) and (7) we get:

$$\varepsilon_M^D + \varepsilon_X^S = -1. \qquad (9)$$

Hence, when $\varepsilon_M^D < -1$, ε_X^S must be positive, i.e. the supply of exports must be upward sloping. When ε_M^D is inelastic $(-1 < \varepsilon_M^D < 0)$, ε_X^S is negative and the supply curve for exports is backward bending.

We have seen that when $\varepsilon_M^D < -1$, the offer curve is positively sloped and when $-1 < \varepsilon_M^D < 0$, it is backward bending. It follows that when the supply of exports is backward bending the offer curve is also backward bending, and that when the supply of exports is upward sloping so too is the offer curve.

The Determination of the Terms of Trade

Offer curves provide information regarding the various precise quantities of exports and imports a country is willing to exchange at various t/t (t_is). However, in the real world at any moment in time, one observes a single t_i, not various t_is. In this section, offer curves are used to determine the equilibrium t_i.

(a) Increasing Opportunity Costs.
     When PPFs exhibit increasing opportunity costs, the offer curves for H and for W have the shape shown in figures 5.12 and 5.14a respectively. The two offer curves are drawn in the same commodity space (figure 5.16) since in a two-country world one country's exports form the other's imports and vice versa. Take, for instance, the terms of trade given by t_1^6. Given t_1^6, H is prepared to import Oc_5 of Clothing in exchange

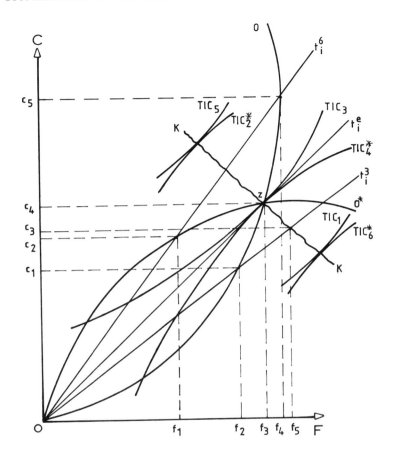

FIG. 5.16

for Of_4 of Food exports. However, W, given t_i^6, is willing to export only Oc_2 of Clothing in exchange for Of_1 of Food imports. Hence t_i^6 reflects an excess supply of Food equal to f_1f_4 and an excess demand for Clothing equal to c_2c_5. This excess demand for Clothing will push the price of Clothing up while the excess supply of Food will depress the price of Food. These two tendencies taken together will lead to a relative rise in the price of Clothing or a relative fall in the price of Food. Hence t_i must become flatter.

Alternatively, given t_i^3, H is prepared to exchange Of_2 of Food exports for Oc_1 of Clothing imports. Given t_i^3, W is willing to import Of_5 of Food in exchange for Oc_4 of Clothing exports. Hence given t_i^3, there is an excess supply of Clothing equal to c_1c_4 and an excess demand for Food equal to f_2f_5. Hence the price of Food will rise and the price of Clothing will fall, i.e. t_i will become steeper.

From this analysis it follows that neither t_i^6 nor t_i^3 is an equilibrium t_i since an equilibrium t_i must clear the market such that the exports of a particular commodity by a country are <u>exactly equal</u> to the other country's imports of it. Given this definition of the equilibrium t_i and having proved that t_i will move clockwise when there is an excess supply of Food accompanied by an excess demand for Clothing and anticlockwise given the contrary situation, it is clear that the equilibrium t_i must be determined by the intersection of the two offer curves: OO and OO*. At point z the quantity of Clothing H is willing to import given t_i^e is equal to Oc_3 and the quantity of Food exports is equal to Of_3. Moreover, given t_i^e, W is prepared to import Of_3 of Food in exchange for Oc_3 exports of Clothing. Hence t_i^e will clear the market since H's exports of Food are equal to W's imports of Food and W's exports of Clothing are equal to H's imports of Clothing. t_i^e is therefore the equilibrium t_i since the international supply of and demand for each of the two commodities are equal. Hence the markets are completely cleared. Note also that from the way we have determined t_i^e, it follows that any other t_i will produce effects that lead back to t_i^e – see section below on multiple equilibria and stability.

In concluding this section we should note that the offer curves are derived by tracing the locus of the points at which TICs are at a tangent to vectors from the origin, i.e. different t_is. This means that more information is given by point z than we have so far discussed. At point z the TICs for H (TIC_3) and for W (TIC_4^*) will be at a tangent to each other, the tangent being t_i^e given the way the offer curves were derived. This means that point z must also lie on the contract curve (KK) where the two sets of TICs are at a tangent to each other (figure 5.16). Hence point z is a point of efficiency since it is superior to any point outside the contract curve. Also note that point z is a point of equilibrium for a world community engaged in free trade, i.e. trade without restrictions of any kind.

(b) Constant Opportunity Costs.

Recall that when PPFs exhibit constant opportunity costs, the offer curves have the shape shown in figures 5.13 and 5.14b. Hence the determination of t_i^e can be achieved in the same manner as before – figure 5.17a. Also note that the intersection of the offer curves need not be in the convex/concave section – figure 5.17b.

Multiple Equilibria and Stability

It has been demonstrated that t_i^e are the equilibrium t_i since

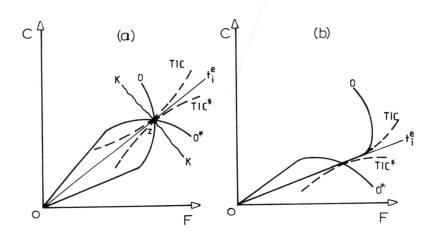

FIG. 5.17

they clear the international market and also because any other t_i will result in forces that take the world economy back to t_i^e. Now assume that the offer curves intersect more than once, i.e. there are multiple equilibria; is it then possible to reach the same categorical conclusions?

In figure 5.18, OO and OO^* have been drawn to intersect three times at points z, z_1 and z_2 hence giving three terms of trade t_i^2, t_i^3 and t_i^1 respectively. All three t_is clear the international market so in that sense they are equilibrium t_is. However, are there any built-in mechanisms that ensure that the world economy will return to the relevant t_i when others around it are being considered? To answer this question, consider t_i^2 and terms of trade around it, t_i^* - not drawn. If t_i is a vector below t_i^2, there will result an excess demand for Clothing accompanied by an excess supply of Food which will, together, raise the price of Clothing relative to that of Food. Hence t_i^* will move in a clockwise direction away from t_i^2. If t_i^* is a vector above t_i^2, there will result an excess supply of Clothing and an excess demand for Food leading to an increase in the relative price of Food. Hence t_i^* will move in an anti-clockwise direction away from t_i^2. Therefore, although t_i^2 clears the international market, any t_i which is different from it will take the world economy away from it. Hence, t_i^2 produces a situation of <u>unstable</u> equilibrium.

Note that any t_i around t_i^2 or t_i^3 will produce forces that

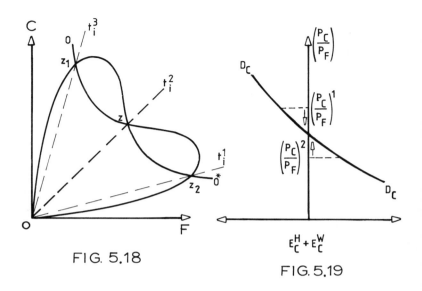

FIG. 5.18

FIG. 5.19

take the international economy back to t_i^1 or t_i^3. Hence t_i^1 and t_i^3 produce situations of <u>stable</u> equilibrium.

The stability conditions can be expressed more formally. From the analysis in the previous sections, the equilibrium market condition for Clothing is given by:

$$E_C^H + E_C^W = 0 \qquad (10)$$

where E is excess demand, i.e. the excess demand for Clothing by H and W is equal to zero. We have seen that E_C^H and E_C^W are both dependent on t_i, i.e. (P_C/P_F). In order to achieve stability it is necessary for the aggregate demand for Clothing $(D_C D_C)$ to be downward sloping when plotted against (P_C/P_F). Hence when t_i is equal to $(P_C/P_F)^1$ (figure 5.19), the aggregate excess demand for Clothing is negative resulting in a fall in t_i and when it is equal to $(P_C/P_F)^2$, the aggregate excess demand is positive leading to a rise in t_i.

The slope of $D_C D_C$ is given by the first derivative of $E_C^H + E_C^W$ with respect to (P_C/P_F). For stability it is necessary for the slope of $D_C D_C$ at the point of equilibrium to be negative:

$$\frac{dE_C^H}{d(P_C/P_F)} + \frac{dE_C^W}{d(P_C/P_F)} < 0 \qquad (11)$$

for the value of (P_C/P_F) determined by 10.

(11) can be rewritten as:

$$\left[\frac{dE_C^H}{d(P_C/P_F)} \frac{P_C/P_F}{E_C^H}\right] \frac{E_C^H}{P_C/P_F} + \left[\frac{dE_C^W}{d(P_C/P_F)} \frac{P_C/P_F}{E_C^W}\right] \frac{E_C^W}{P_C/P_F} < 0 \qquad (12)$$

where the terms in the square brackets are the elasticities of H's demand for imports, $(\varepsilon_M^D)^H$, and W's supply of exports, $(\varepsilon_X^S)^W$. (12) can be simplified to:

$$\frac{1}{P_C/P_F} \left[(\varepsilon_M^D)^H E_C^H + (\varepsilon_X^S)^W E_C^W\right] < 0. \qquad (13)$$

Since P_C/P_F is necessarily positive and since $E_C^H = E_C^W > 0$ from (11), then (13) reduces to:

$$(\varepsilon_M^D)^H - (\varepsilon_X^S)^W < 0. \qquad (14)$$

Recall that Clothing is W's exports and H's imports so it follows that $E_C^H > 0$ and $E_C^W < 0$.

Utilising (9), condition (14) can be restated in terms of H and W's import demand elasticities:

$$(\varepsilon_M^D)^H + (\varepsilon_M^D)^W < -1. \qquad (15)$$

This condition is referred to as the Marshall–Lerner condition. It is both necessary and sufficient for stability. Since both the import demand elasticities are generally negative, the Marshall–Lerner condition states that the sum of the two import demand elasticities in absolute terms must exceed unity. It follows that a sufficient, but not necessary, condition for stability is that the demand for imports by either H or W be elastic at the equilibrium point, i.e. the relevant country's offer curve must be backward bending.

Conclusion

In concluding this chapter it is appropriate to use offer curves and the techniques employed in deriving them to restate the essence of the discussion in chapter 4 on the gains from trading.

Let us use the offer curves for H and W which are derived on the assumption of increasing opportunity costs. Superimpose them on the same commodity space to determine t_I^e (figure 5.20). Then locate the PPFs at their original or autarkic positions as well as at point z at the intersection of the two offer curves OO and OO*. Note that the tangent at X (t_d) has the same slope as the tangent to OO at O and that the slope of the tangent at X* (t_d^*) is equal to the slope of the tangent to OO* at O. The slopes of t_d and t_d^* measure the autarkic relative price ratios for H and W respectively.

Also note that the slopes of the tangents at points X_1 and X_1^* are equal to the slope of t_I^e. This means that H is

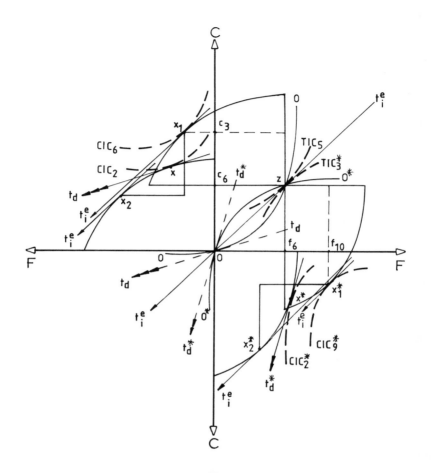

FIG. 5.20

able to move its consumption point from X to X_1 through international trading and that W is able to move its consumption
point from X* to X* for the same reason, i.e. international
trading. However, the locating of the PPFs at point z, which
is a point reached in the process of deriving TICs, is in
effect the equivalent of saying that, given t_i^e which is steeper
than t_d, the equilibrium production point for H will be at X_2
which is along the PPF to the SW of X. The same applies to W
in that t_i^* is flatter than t_d^*, hence X_1^* is equivalent to
another X* point on the PPF for W to the SW of X – X_2^*. What
this really means is that each country is able to adjust its
production as well as its consumption combination to take

advantage of the international t/t: H moves its consumption point from X on CIC_2 to X_1 or CIC_6 and at the same time moves its production point from X to X_2; W moves from X* (on CIC_2^*) to X_1^* (on CIC_9^*) for consumption and from X* to X_2^* for production.

The advantage of plotting the PPFs at point z is to simplify the relationship between production and consumption. At X_1 H plans to produce more Food and less Clothing than it plans to consume — the difference between production and consumption is Of_6 of Food exports and Oc_6 of Clothing imports. W plans to produce more Clothing and less Food than it plans to consume — the difference is Of_6 of Food imports and Oc_6 of Clothing exports. These trade triangles are equivalent to the difference between X_1 and X_2 and X_1^* and X_2^*. Hence **at** point z we are able to highlight the gains from trading via the procedure for determining t_1^e.

We could of course repeat this for the different types of offer curves but that procedure should, by now, be obvious.

Chapter Six

EXPLANATIONS OF THE PATTERN AND COMPOSITION OF INTERNATIONAL
TRADE

Introduction

In chapters 2-5, modern economic techniques were utilised to
demonstrate, albeit under certain restrictive assumptions, how
both 'small' and 'large' countries can benefit from international trade. The rationale rested basically on the understanding that countries export commodities which fetch higher
international (as opposed to domestic) prices and import
commodities which are offered at lower international prices,
i.e. trade takes place when the domestic t/t differ from the
international t/t. These price differences merit special consideration, hence this chapter.

International trade theorists have investigated the back-
ground to differences between domestic and international prices
by attempting to answer questions such as: why do domestic and
international prices differ? why is one country able to produce a commodity more cheaply than another? To answer such
questions meaningfully one needs to analyse the factors that
determine how countries specialise in production and which
commodities are exported and imported.

Several theoretical explanations have been propounded
over the years. At this level of generality it is neither
possible nor desirable to discuss all such explanations. Hence,
this chapter is confined to the most significant postulates:
absolute advantage; comparative advantage; factor abundance;
and the most important recent developments.

Absolute Advantage

This postulate was put forward by Adam Smith (1776) and is
tantamount to stating that a country will export those commodities in which it has an absolute advantage. The explanation of this depends on assuming: (i) a labour theory of value,
i.e. the only cost of production is the number of man hours
(m/h) required per unit of output multiplied by the wage rate
(w); and (ii) that commodity prices are cost-determined. Of

course, the labour theory of value need not be so crude since it can be maintained if capital and other factors of production: (i) are an <u>insignificant</u> part of total production costs; or (ii) have <u>equal</u> significance in all lines of production; or (iii) are accumulated labour-value in the Marxist sense.

Smith further assumed that w is the same in all countries and that different countries require different m/h per unit of output. Hence, differences in production costs, therefore in commodity prices, can be explained in terms of differing m/h requirements. Since the assumption of differing m/h requirements is equivalent to different PFs for the same commodity in different countries, it follows that the principle of absolute advantage amounts to stating that the pattern of trade is determined by differences in factor productivities or in PFs.

Note that in this explanation, once trade takes place there will result complete specialisation in production: each country will specialise completely in the commodity in which it has an absolute advantage, i.e. a lower price. In other words, the PPFs will exhibit characteristics of constant opportunity costs – see chapter 3.

This was a simple, and some would say naive, explanation because international trade theorists are interested in what happens when <u>one</u> country has an absolute advantage in <u>all</u> lines of production. Smith's explanation would seem to rule out trade under such circumstances. However, simple as it is, the principle of absolute advantage can explain the pattern of trade in commodities where the necessary environment or skills are lacking: if a country does not have the appropriate geographical conditions to produce coffee or bananas, it will have to import them since the cost of domestic production would be prohibitive; and if a country does not possess the necessary skilled labour or sophisticated technology to produce a commodity, it will have to import it.

Comparative Advantage

Torrens (1815) and Ricardo (1817) are credited with carrying Smith's doctrine further by analysing the case where one country has an absolute advantage in all lines of production. They assume for each and every country, two commodities (C and F), a single and homogeneous factor of production (L) qualified as in the previous section and constant returns to scale. The autarkic commodity price ratio is then determined by output/factor (a) ratios, if w is the same in all countries. Hence, in a two-country world, if $a_C/a_F > a_C^*/a_F^*$, or $a_C/a_C^* > a_F/a_F^*$, the home country (H) will export commodity C and import commodity F – recall that asterisks refer to the outside world (W). The meaning of this inequality is that international trade is determined by <u>comparative</u> factor productivities or <u>relative</u> output/factor ratios. Note that this proposition is correct even if $a_C > a_C^*$ and $a_F > a_F^*$, i.e. H has an absolute advantage in the production of both commodities. Also note that if the extent of absolute advantage is the same in both commodities no international trade will take place i.e. $a_C/a_F = a_C^*/a_F^*$, or $a_C/a_C^* = a_F/a_F^*$).

This amounts to stating that international trade is determined by comparative rather than absolute advantage. As long as one country is not equally efficient in the production of both commodities, international trade will be beneficial. Needless to add that for every comparative advantage there must exist a comparative disadvantage (a comparative advantage in the production of commodity C for H is simultaneously accompanied by a comparative disadvantage in the production of commodity F for that country), since comparative or relative notions can only exist given a minimum of two countries and two commodities.

The statement that 'international trade is determined by comparative factor productivities' is referred to as the strong statement of the comparative advantage doctrine. This is because only two commodities are considered. However, it is important to know what happens when there are two countries but n commodities. Here one ranks commodities according to their factor productivities such that:

$$a_1/a_1^* > a_2/a_2^* > \ldots \ldots > a_n/a_n^*.$$

Hence it is no longer possible to state categorically that the pattern of trade is determined exclusively by international differences in factor productivities. There is now a chain in which all commodities are ranked according to their comparative factor productivity ratios such that 'it will always be true that a country's exports will have a higher factor productivity ratio than each of its imports'. It is implicit that country H will export commodity 1 and import commodity n. What happens to commodities 2 to n-1 inclusive will depend on the international forces of supply and demand subject to the requirement that the balance of trade must necessarily balance.

The analysis can also be extended to cover m countries as well as n commodities. The interested reader should consult Jones (1961) and Chacholiades (1978, pp. 70-82).

Factor Abundance

Although the principle of comparative advantage takes Smith's analysis a step further, it fails to explain why factor productivities differ between commodities and countries. The next major contribution was concerned with this particular point. The model was advanced, independently, by Heckscher (1919) and Ohlin (1933) but the bulk of rigorous analysis was applied by Samuelson (1948, 1949, 1953, 1965, 1967, etc.). Samuelson's work so developed and transformed the character of the basic model that all international trade theorists find it appropriate to refer to it as the Heckscher-Ohlin-Samuelson

(HOS) model.

The basic HOS model rests on the following assumptions: (i) there are two factors of production (K and L); (ii) there are no transportation costs or trade impediments; (iii) atomistic competition exists in both goods and factor markets; (iv) all PFs are homogeneous of degree 1; (v) there are no factor-intensity reversals; and (vi) PFs are different for different commodities but are the same for any one commodity irrespective of the location of production. Given these assumptions, the HOS model attempts to explain the pattern of trade in terms of relative factor endowments in that it claims that 'factor endowments are the crucial and sole factor to determine comparative advantage'. Some countries are endowed with more K relative to L while others are endowed with more L relative to K and the HOS model suggests that the former group of countries (with $K/L > 1$) will export K-intensive commodities while the latter group (with $K/L < 1$) will export L-intensive commodities. In short: a country will export (import) those commodities which are intensive in the use of its abundant (scarce) factor.

It should be apparent that there are at least two possible interpretations of the term 'factor abundance'. One interpretation defines factor abundance in terms of prices: a country's abundant factor is its cheaper factor so that if H is K-abundant, $P_K/P_K^* < 1$ where P stands for price per unit. The other interpretation defines factor abundance in physical terms so that $K/K^* > 1$ if H is K-abundant relative to W.

What are the implications of the different interpretations? First, consider the price definition of abundance. If: $P_K/P_L < P_K^*/P_L^*$, i.e. H has relatively cheaper K while W has relatively cheaper L, H is K-abundant while W is L-abundant. Now consider figure 6.1 where C_1 and F_1 are the respective isoquants for one unit of commodities C and F. The isoquants are drawn in such a way that commodity C is K-intensive while commodity F is L-intensive at all possible factor-price ratios. Recalling that PFs are homogeneous of degree 1 and that there are no factor-intensity reversals, it follows that these two isoquants are typical of their set — see chapter 3. From the assumption that H has cheaper K and more expensive L (reflected in the slope of K_3L_1) and W has cheaper L and more expensive K (reflected in the slope of lines such as K_2L_3 or K_0L_2 which are flatter than K_3L_1), one can calculate the relative cost of producing a unit of C and F in both H and W.

Take H whose relative factor prices are given by K_3L_1. From point Z_1, giving the optimum factor combination for a unit of commodity C, it can be seen that a unit of C costs $OK_1 + OL_0$. Since OL_0 (= K_1Z_1) can be bought for K_3L_1, it follows that a unit of C costs OK_3 in H. Alternatively, it can be shown that one unit of C costs OL_1 since OK_1 (= L_0Z_1) can be exchanged for L_0L_1. Also a unit of commodity F can be shown, following the same procedure, to cost either OK_3 or OL_1. Therefore, in

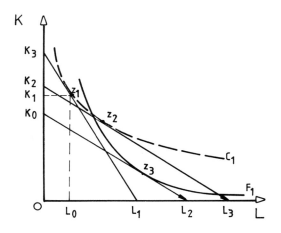

FIG. 6.1

H a unit of C costs the same as a unit of F. Given the assumption that commodity prices (P_X and P_Y) are cost-determined, it also follows that: $P_C/P_F = 1$.

Now in W, following exactly the same procedure, it can be demonstrated that a unit of C costs either OK_2 or OL_3 while a unit of F costs either OK_0 or OL_2. Hence, in W: $P_C^*/P_F^* > 1$. Therefore, $P_C/P_F < P_C^*/P_F^*$. In other words, H can offer commodity C at a lower price than W, while W can offer commodity F more cheaply than H. Hence H will export commodity C and import commodity F while W will export commodity F and import commodity C. This is the same as stating that H will export the K-intensive commodity and import the L-intensive commodity with the contrary applying to W. Since the starting point was that H is K-abundant, the proposition has therefore been vindicated.

Now, consider the alternative definition of abundance. If H is K-abundant while W is L-abundant in the physical sense, it follows that: $K/L > K^*/L^*$. It is no longer possible to follow the previous procedure since physical abundance does not tell much about factor prices. In figure 6.2, HH and WW are the respective PPFs for H and W. HH and WW have been drawn in such a way that the K-abundant (L-abundant) country, H(W), can produce more C(F). If it is assumed that both countries consume the two commodities in similar (not necessarily exact) proportions, i.e. their demand patterns are similar,

78

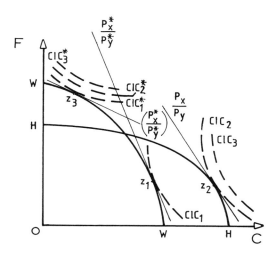

FIG. 6.2

one can depict their preferences by one set of community indifference curves: CIC_1, CIC_2, etc. Hence, in autarky, the
commodity price ratio in H is P_C/P_F while that in W is P_C^*/P_F^*.
Since H's autarkic price ratio is steeper than W's, it follows
that: $P_C/P_F < P_C^*/P_F^*$. Therefore, the HOS proposition remains
valid since this relationship implies that H(W) will export
commodity C(F) and import commodity F(C), hence the K-abundant
(L-abundant) country will export the K-intensive (L-intensive)
commodity, thus vindicating the HOS proposition.

However, if consumer preferences in H are those depicted
by CIC_1, CIC_2, etc. while those in W are depicted by CIC_1^*,
CIC_2^*, etc., it can be seen that W's autarkic commodity price
ratio is flatter than H's. Hence $P_C/P_F > P_C^*/P_F^*$. Therefore,
H will export commodity F and import commodity C while W will
export commodity C and import commodity F. In other words,
the K-abundant country will export the L-intensive commodity
and the L-abundant country will export the K-intensive commodity. Hence the HOS hypothesis is refuted.

From this analysis it becomes clear that when factor
abundance is defined in physical terms, a necessary condition
for vindicating the HOS proposition is that the two countries
have broadly similar demand patterns. If each country is
biased in its consumption towards the commodity which is intensive in the use of its physically abundant factor, that
factor need not be the cheaper factor (recall that the demand

for factors is a derived demand – see chapter 3) and the HOS proposition is nullified. Needless to add, the price definition of abundance simply dodges the issue since factor prices are themselves determined by the relevant supply and demand forces.

In concluding this section, it should be pointed out that the HOS model can be generalised to many countries, many commodities and many factors. The analysis becomes complicated, however, and the interested reader should consult Chipman (1966), Vanek (1968) and Chacholiades (1978, pp. 286-94).

Vent for Surplus

The 'vent for suplus' theory is intended to provide an understanding of the implications of international trade for colonial countries, particularly those in S.E. Asia. However, the theory has a general application to most developing countries.

The theory is based on the premise that in autarky a country has 'disguised' unemployment in land and labour, implying the existence of a plentiful potential supply of the two factors of production. The 'disguised' unemployment is due to the abundance of natural resources and the low opportunity cost of leisure which, together, provide an explanation for the high labour productivity in Food relative to Clothing leading to production inside the country's PPF. Therefore, when the country is 'opened up' for trade, it can expand its production of Food without curtailing its output of Clothing. This is because the international t/t raise the opportunity cost of leisure relative to work, hence leading to a better utilisation of both land and labour. Therefore, international trade provides a 'vent' for the surplus labour and land (see Myint 1958).

When the country reaches its full potential (by producing along the PPF), the usual analysis then applies. This is therefore not a theory, rather an explanation of the implications of free trade when a country initially produces inside its PPF. There is therefore no need to take it further.

Empirical Evidence?

The comparative advantage and factor endowment postulates have been empirically tested. MacDougall (1951, 1952 and 1962) was the first to attempt a statistical investigation of the validity of the comparative advantage doctrine. His pioneering efforts were followed by others, for example, Stern (1962), Balassa (1963), Bhagwati (1964) and Agarwal, et al (1975). With regard to the predictions of the HOS model, the pioneering attempt was made by Leontief (1953 and 1956) and his work stimulated contributions from, inter alia, Tarshis (1954), Tatemoto and Ichimura (1959), Wahl (1961), Stolper and

Roskamp (1961), Bharadwaj (1962), and Baldwin (1971).

MacDougall studied American (USA) and British (UK) exports of similar groups of commodities. Since he was testing the comparative advantage hypothesis, he predicted that the country with the lower comparative labour costs for any group of commodities would be the exporter of that commodity. However, in the case of USA and UK exports in 1937 (the latest year for which MacDougall had reasonable data), bilateral trade was only a small percentage of their total trade, since the bulk of their exports went to third markets: "more than 95% of British exports of all our sample products but three, more than 95% of American exports of the products but six" (MacDougall 1951, p. 699). Also, the level of mutual tariffs distorted mutual trade. MacDougall, therefore, attempted to test the extent to which the export shares of the USA and the UK to third markets were related to each country's comparative labour cost position vis-a-vis the other.

Recall that the comparative advantage hypothesis is based on the assumption that w is the same in all countries. However, in 1937, in USA manufacturing w was twice as high as in the UK. MacDougall therefore predicted:

   (i)   if USA labour productivity is twice as high as that of the UK, the two countries will share exports equally;
   (ii) if USA labour productivity is more than twice that of the UK, the USA will dominate the markets; and
   (iii) if USA labour productivity is less than twice that of the UK, the latter will dominate the market.

In short, MacDougall attempted to test the following hypotheses:

(i) a_i^{UK}/a_i^{USA} is positively correlated with E_i^{UK}/E_i^{USA} where $i = 1, \ldots, k$, a as previously and E is share of exports,

(ii) if $\dfrac{1/a_i^{UK}}{1/a_i^{USA}} \cdot \dfrac{w_i^{UK}}{w_i^{USA}} > 1$ (i.e. the factor output ratio times w is higher in the UK than in the USA), it follows that $E_i^{UK}/E_i^{USA} < 1$; and (iii) $\dfrac{1/a_i^{UK}}{1/a_i^{USA}} \cdot \dfrac{w_i^{UK}}{w_i^{USA}}$ is negatively correlated with E_i^{UK}/E_i^{USA}.

MacDougall tested these hypotheses on 25 groups of commodities most of which were manufactured and semi-manufactured goods. Of the 25, 20 (97 per cent of the value of the total sample) were consistent with the prediction with a coefficient of correlation of 0.8. The remaining groups became consistent when a different definition of labour productivity was applied. However, although the dividing line in terms of export shares was expected to be where USA productivity was twice that of the UK, it was found to be 2.5 times. MacDougall explained this in terms of: the UK's commercial reputation in third countries in 1937; her extensive financial networks at the time; her influence in overseas territories; and 'imperial preference' (now 'commonwealth preference') where members of the Commonwealth gained relatively freer access to each other's markets.

Later studies confirmed these results. For example, Stern (1962) used 1950 data when w in the USA was about $3\frac{1}{2}$ times that of the UK. He found that when USA labour productivity was $3\frac{1}{2}$ times that of the UK, USA exports to third markets were still less than the UK's, but this factor had risen from 2/5th to 4/5th. This lends support to MacDougall's clarification since by 1950 the advantages enjoyed by the UK in 1937 were being gradually eroded.

These studies were attacked very vigorously by Bhagwati (1964 or 1969). Bhagwati emphasised that each of the three hypotheses tested by MacDougall had two basic elements: (i) the adequacy of the labour productivity ratios as a proxy to price ratios; and (ii) the relation of price ratios to quantity ratios in third countries. Bhagwati asserted that only (i) relates to the comparative advantage doctrine while differences in preferences, qualities, distance and historical and cultural links ensure that (ii) does not. Moreover, Bhagwati conducted his own tests and found no correlation between labour productivity ratios and price ratios. It is relative prices that should determine relative export shares. Although neither MacDougall's nor Bhagwati's studies can be easily discarded (each side has a large literature purporting to support it), the only sensible conclusion is that the evidence is inconclusive.

In attempting to evaluate empirically the HOS hypothesis, Leontief asked: what would be the effect on the use of K and L in the USA if total exports and imports were each reduced by $1m and the previously imported commodities replaced by similar commodities produced domestically? That is, he deliberately excluded from his analysis commodities for which no import-competing industries existed in the USA, e.g. coffee, bananas, etc. He asked the question in this way simply because the analysis had to be confined to USA data since no such data were available for a country with which the USA conducted a large proportion of her international trade. Therefore, he wanted to use the K/L ratio in USA import-competing industries as a proxy to that ratio in exporting countries - a legitimate procedure if one recalls that the HOS model assumes that the same commodity is subject to the same PF in all countries.

The distribution of the $1m worth of exports and imports over specific commodity sectors was made in proportion to the importance of these sectors in total exports and imports. Leontief then used his input-output technique, employing 1947 data (the latest available) to estimate the amount of production from each sector of the economy that would be required (both directly and indirectly) for the $1m worth of exports and imports distributed in this way. He then calculated the K and L inputs needed for these levels of production. These were calculated from the input-coefficient matrix. These sectoral estimates were then added up to give the figures for the total K and L required for the $1m worth of exports and import-substitutes. The final result showed the USA to export L-intensive commodities and to import K-intensive commodities.

Since all economists, including Leontief, believed that the USA was K-abundant, Leontief's results came as a complete surprise, not least to Leontief himself; hence the term 'the Leontief Paradox'; the results seemed an outright refutation of the HOS hypothesis that K-abundant countries will export K-intensive goods.

There is a massive literature containing similar studies for other countries (some producing empirical support for the HOS predictions and some contradicting them) and critiques of Leontief's study. The critiques concentrate on: the choice of year; statistical problems; the HOS assumptions; etc. There is no need to discuss these here since some studies are based on assumptions which were empirically refuted later and some are simply not worth the paper they were written on. The most significant of these studies, however, are those relating to the 'proper' choice of the factors of production. The USA was initially abundantly endowed with natural resources, but intensive industrialisation and economic development have made these gifts of nature relatively scarce. Hence the USA now imports commodities which are intensive in their use of natural resources and exports commodities which are relatively intensive in their use of both K and L. Moreover, many industries which use natural resources (e.g. farming, coal mining) are also K-intensive. Therefore, the USA's imports of natural resources make its overall imports K-intensive simply because of this basic reality. Once this is realised the 'paradox' disappears altogether: indeed empirical evidence supports this idea - see, inter alia, Vanek (1959).

Recent Developments

Following the work of MacDougall and Leontief emerged a number of new theoretical explanations of the pattern of international trade:

(i) Kravis (1956) suggested that international trade is confined to commodities which are not available domestically. Unavailability could be interpreted in an absolute sense, for example a country which has no gold or diamond deposits will have to import them. But it could also be interpreted in the sense that domestic supply of a commodity is inelastic so that expanding domestic production would entail relatively higher costs. Kravis justifies his theory by stating that impediments on trade, transportation costs, cartelisation and similar factors eliminate from international trade goods which can be produced domestically, albeit at a relatively higher cost. In short, unavailability could be due to a relative lack of natural resources or to the ability of innovating countries to have a temporary monopoly in a differentiated product in which they happen to acquire the necessary technical skills.

(ii) Linder (1961), who made a distinction between trade in manufactured and primary products, suggested that trade in primary products can be explained in terms of the HOS model by relative natural resource endowments while trade in manufactured products needs a different rationale. He suggested that the "volume of trade in manufactures of a country with each of her trading partners, when taken as a proportion of the corresponding national incomes of these countries, will be higher, the greater the similarity in the demand patterns of the pair of trading countries" (Bhagwati 1960 or 1969, p.37). Unfortunately, the similarity of demand patterns has come to be interpreted in terms of per capita incomes rather than cultural and broad economic considerations: is it really conceivable that Kuwait and the USA (with similar per capita incomes) will experience increasing bilateral trade relative to their total trade?

(iii) Kenen (1965 and 1970) and Keesing (1968) attempted to explain international trade in terms of 'human skills'. The postulate here is that countries relatively well endowed with skilled labour will export commodities which are intensive in their use of skilled labour while countries relatively well endowed with unskilled labour will export commodities which are intensive in their use of unskilled labour. As should be apparent, this postulate is tantamount to a restatement of the HOS hypothesis in terms of a refined factor classification.

(iv) Posner (1961) and Vernon (1966) proposed an explanation of international trade which is attributable to 'technological gaps'. They postulated that a country which succeeds in innovating a commodity or a production process may develop a temporary monopoly in the relevant technological expertise. Consequently that country will either increase its volume of exports of that product or reduce its volume of imports of it. This is a Schumpetarian type of explanation suggesting that a country's monopoly will last for as long as it takes other countries to successfully 'imitate' its innovation. In a dynamic world of ever increasing innovations, the gap between innovation and imitation is adequate to explain a dynamic pattern of trade.

(v) Vernon (1966) and Hirsch (1967) proposed a 'life-cycle' hypothesis. This rests on the notion that the factor combination necessary for the production of a commodity may alter over that commodity's life-cycle: the techniques of production for a new commodity may be at an experimental stage, hence they may need quite frequent alterations in design, specifications, etc. During the early stages, the factor combination may entail relatively large amounts of skilled labour and small quantities of K. When the product reaches a mature stage, stable and longer-run techniques will be introduced with the consequence that the required quantity of K will increase relative to the amount of skilled labour. Hence, the imports of a relatively less successful innovating nation will be increasingly dominated by new products while its exports will be increasingly dominated by mature products, with the implication that over a long period of time the country will find the skill-intensity of its imports rising relative to that of its exports, while the K-intensity of its imports will decrease relative to that of its exports - see Katrak (1982).

(vi) Grubel and Lloyd (1975) suggested that the combination of product differentiation, differences in tastes and economies of scale means that a country may export and import the same broad category of commodities (e.g. the UK both exports and imports cars) and their empirical work provides evidence that this is a fairly common characteristic of trade between advanced nations. From this, it follows that their proposition refers to intra-industry as opposed to inter-industry trade. Note that this proposition rests on altering three of the assumptions on which the HOS model is built: (a) the assumption of homogeneous products is replaced by differentiated products; (b) the assumption of constant returns to scale is replaced by increasing returns to scale; and (c) the assumption of similar demand patterns is replaced by differences in demand patterns. It is therefore fundamentally different from the basic HOS model. However, this does not mean that it contradicts it, rather that it enriches the HOS model by realistically changing some of its basic premises: a moment's reflection should be enough to demonstrate that the changing of two of the three elements just stated will lend support to the HOS predictions.

Conclusion

A whole book could be devoted to a discussion of new theories purporting to explain the pattern of international trade. This is particularly so when transportation costs and non-traded goods such as defence, education and national health are incorporated into the analysis (see chapters 9 and 11), but at this level of generality that is neither feasible nor desirable.

In concluding this chapter it should be stressed that the cursory discussion here has been deliberate. This author has always preached that no single theory is capable of explaining international trade in all commodities at all times. Hence, the seemingly unsatisfactory state of inconclusion reached in this chapter is very welcome: international trade theorists should never again contemplate grand theoretical structures; they should confine their analysis to manageable and realistic aspects of the subject.

Chapter Seven

ISSUES EMANATING FROM THE HOS MODEL

Introduction

The HOS model, which was explained and discussed in the previous chapter, attributes differences in autarkic commodity
prices to divergencies in autarkic factor prices. Also, it
was demonstrated in chapter 4 that free international trade is
beneficial to countries engaging in it since the international
equalisation of commodity prices enables each country to specialise in the commodity in which it has a comparative advantage. Moreover, it was shown in chapter 3 that any change in
the combined production of the two commodities entails certain
changes in factor prices, hence in factor rewards. The combination of these statements raises two interesting issues:
firstly, given the HOS model, one needs to know what happens
to factor prices as a result of the complete equalisation of
international commodity prices made possible by free trade and
lack of transportation costs; secondly, since the HOS model
postulates that a country will export commodities which are
intensive in their use of the country's abundant factor, one
needs to investigate what happens to the two factors of production in conditions of both free and restricted trade in
comparison with the autarkic situation.

These two issues have been the inspiration of two theorems: the factor price equalisation theorem (Samuelson 1948
and 1949) and the Stolper-Samuelson theorem (Stolper and
Samuelson 1941). Moreover, there is a third issue which,
though not directly related to these two theorems, also emanates from the HOS model: one should be interested to know what
happens to the production of the two commodities when a country
experiences a change in its factor endowment. The investigation of this issue has led to the Rybczynski theorem
(Rybczynski, 1955). This chapter is devoted to a brief discussion of these theorems.

Issues Emanating from the HOS Model

The Factor Price Equalisation Theorem

The HOS model is based on assumptions which include perfect
factor mobility within each nation but perfect immobility
internationally. If factors of production were perfectly
mobile between nations, perfect competition in factor and
commodity markets would automatically guarantee the complete
equalisation of factor prices internationally. The interesting question arises as to whether or not the complete lack of
factor mobility internationally can be compensated for by the
complete equalisation of commodity prices made possible by
free trade in the absence of any transportation costs. In
other words, is it likely that the international free exchange
of commodities could result in the elimination of international
differences in factor payments?

To answer this question meaningfully, one needs to recall
the assumptions of the HOS model which were stated in the
previous chapter. The assumptions enable one to construct
figure 7.1 where the box O_FBO_CD represents the home country's
(H's) given endowment of labour (L) and capital (K) and the
box $O_FAO_C^*E$ represents the given factor endowment for the rest
of the world (W). The production of Food (F) and Clothing (C)
is measured from the origin or corner of the relevant box
(O_F, O_C and O_C^*), with asterisks denoting elements relating to
W.

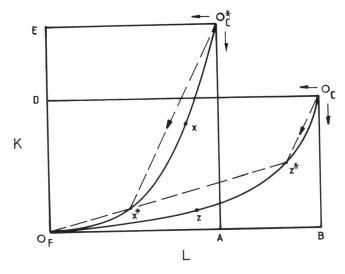

FIG. 7.1

Figure 7.1 has been drawn such that the length O_FE
exceeds O_FD while the length of O_FB exceeds O_FA, i.e. the
sizes of the two boxes indicate that H is a L-abundant country
while W is K-abundant, using the physical definition of abundance. Since the two boxes have a common corner or origin at
O_F, the production of F is measured from that origin for both
H and W. Hence the F isoquants (not drawn) apply to both
countries which is consistent with the assumption of identical
PFs. Also, the C isoquants (not drawn) relating to the
origins O_C and O_C^* must be the same, i.e. if O_C and O_C^* were to
coincide, the isoquants would be identical. Note that the
diagram has been drawn to show F as the L-intensive and C as
the K-intensive industry in both countries without any factor-
intensity reversals – the contract curves (O_FO_C and $O_FO_C^*$) lie
consistently below the relevant diagonal.

In autarky, H is producing at point z and W at point x.
Recall that the respective vectors (not drawn) from O_F, O_C and
O_C^* to z and x measure the factor intensities as well as the
factor productivities, given the assumptions of homogeneous
PFs of degree 1 and constant returns to scale. Hence the
tangents to the isoquants at these points measure the ratio of
the wage rate (w) to the price of capital (π) – factor price
ratio (w/π). From the diagram it can be seen that H (compared
with   W) uses more L-intensive methods in the production of
both F and C – O_FO_C lies consistently below $O_FO_C^*$ except, of
course, at the origin O_F. Hence, the marginal productivity of
L at z is lower than that of L at x. Since the contrary is
true for K, it follows that w is lower in H and π is lower in
W.

Since z and x are the autarkic production points, it
follows that the autarkic price (P) ratios are such that:
$P_L/P_K < P_L^*/P_K^*$. Given the HOS postulate, with free trade H
will expand its production of F and export it and will contract
its production of C and import it, while W will do the appropriate opposite – the final result being that commodity prices
(P_F and P_C) are equalised. Now, suppose that this pattern of
change results in z* and x* as the new respective production
points for H and W such that z* and x* lie along the same
vector from O_F and along parallel vectors from O_C and O_C^*.
This means that the factor intensities in F become identical
in both H and W with the same being true in the case of C,
i.e. free trade is depicted as resulting in identical factor
intensities for each commodity internationally.

Since the HOS model assumes constant returns to scale, it
follows that the marginal productivities of K and L are constant along any ray from the origin – see chapter 3. Given
that points z* and x* lie along the same vector from O_F and
parallel vectors from O_C and O_C^*, it follows that factor productivities, hence factor prices, have been completely equalised internationally as a result of free trade without transportation costs, i.e. as a result of complete commodity price

equalisation. Hence the complete lack of international factor mobility has been totally compensated for by the complete equalisation of commodity prices internationally.

One needs to ask about the likelihood of finding points such as z^* and x^* since a movement of z towards z^* (without reaching it) and x towards x^* (without reaching it) will simply indicate a narrowing in factor price divergencies rather than complete factor price equalisation. It should be apparent that complete specialisation in production will rule out such a possibility - if H produces at O_C and W at O_F the factor intensities, hence factor prices, will be determined by the diagonals $O_F O_C$ and $O_F O_C^*$. Also, it should be apparent that larger divergencies in the factor endowment ratios will preclude such possibilities.

To conclude this section one needs to consider the economic rationale for this technical discussion. In autarky, H had cheaper L relative to K, with the opposite holding true for W. With free trade, H exports F, the L-intensive commodity, and imports C, the K-intensive commodity. This is made possible by expanding production of F and contracting that of C. However, the L and K released by contracting the production of C are in the wrong proportion required for expanding the production of F - more K is released relative to L. Hence both industries need to be persuaded to use more K than previously. This can be achieved only by lowering π relative to w - see chapter 3. Hence, free trade raises the price of the abundant factor and lowers the price of the scarce factor. Since appropriate changes are happening simultaneously in W, it follows that free trade narrows the autarkic factor price differentials. Whether or not these differentials are completely eliminated will depend on the specific factors mentioned earlier.

In reality, the considerations raised at the end of the previous chapter together with the existence of some factor mobility internationally plus lack of factor homogeneity make it impossible to predict with any degree of precision the impact of free trade on factor prices. Hence, one should beware of any dogmatic practical assertions regarding this issue.

The Stolper-Samuelson Theorem

Given the analysis in chapter 3, the Stolper-Samuelson theorem can be briefly explained with   reference to figure 3.8. Suppose free international trade resulted in production at point x_4 while restricted trade (due to imposition of a tariff or a similar trade impediment - see chapter 8), which raised the domestic price of C, resulted in production at point x_2. Hence the move from x_4 to x_2 is due to a rise in the commodity price ratio P_C/P_F. Since in that diagram C is K-intensive while F is L-intensive, the move from x_4 to x_2 releases K and L from the contracting F industry in the wrong proportion required in the expanding C industry. To be precise, more L is released than is appropriate. Hence both industries have to be persuaded to use more L than before if L and K are to be fully employed. This can be achieved only by lowering w relative to π, i.e. a fall in the factor price ratio w/π.

Now, since the move from x_4 to x_2 requires an absolute increase in the output of C and since in the process of generating this expanded output π has risen and given that C is K-intensive, it follows that K has become better off as a result of this move while L has become worse off absolutely. However, this conclusion is not dependent on assuming that the total value of production (i.e national income) is measured in terms of C only since all that matters is that π rises in both industries (ensured by the assumption of perfect factor mobility within each country): given the total endowment of K, the raising of π to π_1 ensures that the total reward to K (i.e. $K\pi_1$) increases in absolute terms - $K\pi < K\pi_1$. Since w has been lowered in the process to w_1 in both industries, it follows that $Lw > Lw_1$. Hence L is worse off in absolute terms.

This conclusion remains intact as long as all the assumptions on which the box diagram is constructed remain valid and provided the imposition of trade impediments raises the domestic price of the affected commodity. If these assumptions are no longer valid, the conclusion may be nullified or even reversed. A full appreciation of these considerations requires familiarity with tariff analysis - see chapters 8-10.

In concluding this section it is appropriate to state the conclusion of this theorem more rigorously and to relate it to the HOS model. The Stolper-Samuelson theorem postulates that if the price of a commodity rises, and this commodity is L-(K-) intensive, not only does w (π) rise, but w(π) also rises to a proportionately greater extent than the price of the commodity, hence the factor payment buys more of any commodity than previously: L(K) is better off in real terms.

How does this relate to the HOS model? Since in the HOS model free trade benefits the abundant factor by expanding the production of the commodity that is intensive in its use, it follows that any impediment on trade which restricts the production of that commodity must benefit the factor least intensively used in that commodity - the country's less abundant factor. That is why the Stolper-Samuelson theorem is an issue that emanates from the HOS model.

The Rybczynski Theorem

The Rybczynski theorem predicts that an increase in the endowment of a factor (the other factor endowment remaining constant) necessarily causes the output of the industry which is intensive in its use to expand and the output of the other industry to contract. More precisely, an increase in the

endowment of L(K) must cause an expansion in the output of the
L-(K-) intensive industry and a contraction in the output of
the K-(L-) intensive industry.

The proof of this theorem is straightforward when one
assumes constant commodity prices before and after the increase
in the endowment of the factor. This is because constant
commodity prices imply constant factor productivities, hence
constant factor prices, i.e. the factor proportions in the two
industries must remain at their initial levels. This assumption makes it possible to construct a simple diagram like
figure 7.2. In this diagram the initial factor endowment is
that given by the size of the box O_FAO_CB and production is at
point z. The lengths of O_Fz and O_Cz give the respective F and
C outputs.

Assuming there is an increase in the endowment of L of AC,
the factor endowment box becomes $O_FCO_C'B$. The production point
now becomes z_1, given the assumption of constant factor prices:
point z_1 must lie along the same vector O_Fz for F production
as well as along a vector parallel to O_Cz ($O_C'z_1$) – see
chapter 3.

Given that the output of F and C can be measured by the
length of the vector from the relevant origin (due to the
assumption of linear homogeneous PFs of degree 1), figure 7.2
shows that at point z_1 the output of F has increased by the
length of the distance zz_1. The figure also shows the vector
$O_C'z_1$ to be shorter than the vector O_Cz (if one were to draw a

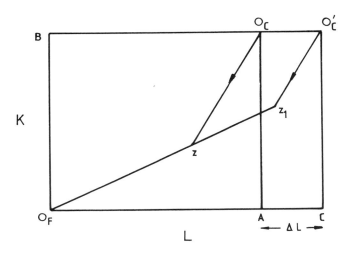

FIG. 7.2

91

horizontal line from z_1 to cross O_Cz at point x – not indicated – the vectors $O_C'z_1$ and O_Cx would be equal in length),
hence the output of C has contracted. Since in figure 7.2 F
is depicted as L–intensive and C as K–intensive, it follows
that the increment in the endowment of L has resulted in an
absolute expansion in the output of F and an absolute contraction in the output of C. Hence, the Rybczynski theorem is
vindicated.

The economic rationale of the theorem is also straightforward. Since commodity prices are to remain constant,
factor proportions have to be maintained at their initial
levels. Now, the only way to guarantee full utilisation of
the increased endowment of L is obviously by expanding the
L–intensive industry. However, given that the K/L ratio in F
must remain constant, the expansion of F will require some K.
Since the extra K can be acquired only from the K–intensive C
industry, that industry must contract. But if the C industry
is to contract and still maintain its K/L ratio, it will re-
lease both K and L at that ratio. Hence the K/L ratio released will be in excess of that required in the F industry,
therefore more of the newly endowed L can be added to the released K and L to bring the ratio to the level required in F
production. This process should be carried to the point where
the combination of the newly endowed L and the released K and
L give a K/L ratio exactly equal to that required in F production. Hence, the output of C must contract absolutely and
the output of F must expand absolutely if the assumption of
constant commodity and factor prices is to be upheld.

It is useful to conclude this discussion by considering
various possible changes in factor endowment in order to give
the theorem a wider perspective. For instance, if there is an
increment in the endowment of both K and L and this change in
endowment is equal to the national factor proportion, the new
endowment box will be determined by O_F, as one corner, and a
corner that lies along an extension of the diagonal O_FO_C to
the north–east of O_C. It is then apparent that if commodity
prices remain constant, both F and C output will increase at
the same rate, i.e. the production effect will be neutral.
Alternatively, using the Rybczynski case (i.e. extending O_C
horizontally to O_C' as in figure 7.2) and this case (i.e.
extending O_C along O_FO_C to reach O_C' – not drawn) as extreme
cases, one can depict intermediate cases where O_C' lies along a
line from O_C to the north–east drawn parallel to O_Fz or along
an extension of zO_C, but the implications for the outputs of F
and C should be too obvious to deserve any specific consideration.

Chapter Eight

IMPEDIMENTS ON TRADE

Introduction

It was demonstrated in chapter 4 that free international trade, given certain restrictive assumptions, is the best regime for the world in that it increases countries' potential welfare. It is therefore pertinent to ask why it is that nations erect impediments on their trade. To answer this question one needs to be familiar with the branch of trade theory generally referred to as the theory of trade (commercial) policy.

It should be stressed from the start that trade impediments take a variety of forms: the imposition of tariffs, import quota restrictions, export subsidies, differing industrial standards, etc. (see Baldwin 1971). To simplify discussion such impediments can be reduced to: tariffs, quotas and 'other' instruments (usually referred to as hidden trade barriers). Furthermore, all trade restrictions except tariffs are known as non-tariff trade distortions.

However, most discussion of this subject has been conducted in terms of tariffs. The reason is that tariffs are the device most widely used for regulating trade flows. Moreover, except under very special circumstances, tariffs are practically the only measure of trade regulation permitted by GATT. Finally, tariffs operate via the price mechanism, hence the analysis of tariffs can easily be extended to incorporate any trade impediments that operate via the price mechanism.

Reasons for Tariffs

In one of his many formidable contributions to the theory of tariffs, the late Professor Johnson (1965) stated that the arguments as to why countries impose tariffs on trade fall into three general categories: economic arguments; non-economic arguments; and non-arguments. By non-economic arguments one means socio-political considerations and similar rationales - for instance, a country may deem it necessary for its long term survival (the preservation of a certain way of life;

military independence; security of food supplies; etc.) to be less dependent on trade by being more autarkic. Amongst economic arguments is the existence of a divergence between private and social costs and benefits – it will be remembered that the rationale for free international trade was provided in terms of private costs and benefits only. Finally, non-arguments simply refer to fallacies or misconceptions regarding the economic consequences of tariff imposition.

The aim of this chapter is, therefore, to analyse the effects of tariffs and to compare these with the effects of a quota restriction as an example of non-tariff trade distortion. Further considerations will be introduced in the next chapter, and these will make it possible to discuss one example of each of the three categories of arguments just mentioned.

Effects of Tariffs

Before discussing the subject in more depth, it should be stressed that tariffs could be specific, ad valorem or a combination of the two (compound duties). A specific tariff is simply what it says, for example £X collected as a duty per car imported irrespective of the total number of cars, while an ad valorem tariff is levied as a percentage of the total value of the imported item. Since a specific tariff can easily be calculated as a percentage rate, the analysis here will be conducted entirely in ad valorem terms.

To analyse the economic effects of tariff imposition, consider a partial equilibrium diagram (figure 8.1) where $P_W S_W$ is W's perfectly elastic supply function for commodity C (i.e. at price OP_W consumers in H can buy any quantity they wish), SS is H's domestic supply curve and DD is its domestic demand curve. Under free trade conditions, H plans to consume Oq_4, produce (domestically) Oq_1 and import the difference $(q_1 q_4)$ from W at a total cost of $q_1 A B q_4$ (= $q_1 q_4$ x OP_W).

Assuming that tariffs do not affect the terms of trade (i.e. H's demand for and supply of commodity C have no effect on world prices) and that tariffs are completely translated into an increase in the price facing H's consumers, the imposition of a tariff (t) raises the domestic price to OP_W^t (i.e. shifts W's supply curve up to $P_W^t S_W^t$). As a result planned consumption falls by $q_3 q_4$ (from Oq_4 to Oq_3), domestic production expands by $q_1 q_2$ (from Oq_1 to Oq_2) and the level of imports falls to $q_2 q_3$ (from $q_1 q_4$). Hence the tariff imposition is equivalent to a tax on the domestic consumer accompanied by a subsidy to the domestic producer.

In partial equilibrium terms, these are the basic effects of tariff imposition, hence it is important to consider their implications carefully. For H, as a society of consumers, the fall in consumption from Oq_4 to Oq_3 results in a decrease in consumers' surplus by area $P_W P_W^t CB$. However, H, as a society of producers, experiences an increase in producers' surplus by

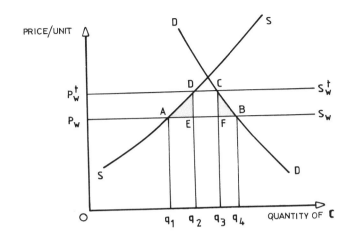

FIG. 8.1

area $P_W P_W^t DA$ as a result of expanding domestic production by $q_1 q_2$ - this is called the redistribution effect. Moreover, the quantity of imports from W after tariff imposition ($q_2 q_3$) costs $q_2 EF q_3$ but the domestic consumers pay $q_2 DC q_3$ with the difference (area EDCF) accruing to the government as tariff revenue. Assuming that the tariff revenue is spent by the government at the same marginal valuation as that at which the consumers give it up (i.e. there is no accusation that one can spend one's money better than the government), it follows that area EDCF is simply a transfer between the private and public sectors of the community without any significant welfare consequences. Hence, the balance sheet of effects is such that $P_W P_W^t CB$ is a welfare loss part of which accrues to producers as surplus ($P_W P_W^t DA$) and part (EDCF) to the government as tariff revenue. Therefore, there is a dead-weight loss given by the shaded triangles (ADE plus FCB). The tariff imposition, given the specified assumptions, therefore results in a net welfare loss for the country imposing it. Moreover, the tariff harms W, the country exporting to H, by reducing its exports by $q_1 q_2$ plus $q_3 q_4$, but in partial-equilibrium terms these are too insignificant to be noticed - see next section on general equilibrium.

These dead-weight losses need careful consideration. The quantity $q_1 q_2$ can be bought from W at a cost of $q_1 AE q_2$ but to produce it domestically costs $q_1 AD q_2$ - the sum of the marginal costs depicted by SS. Hence, in order to attract the necessary resources to produce this extra domestic output H incurs a mis-allocation of resources at a cost of area ADE. The quantity q_3q_4 gives the consumers a total welfare indicated by area q_3CBq_4 but its cost to them is only q_3FBq_4. However, the tariff imposition, in reducing consumption by q_3q_4, results in welfare losses of that area (q_3CBq_4) but consumers can spend the amount q_3FBq_4 on another commodity, hence the dead-weight loss is the area FCB only.

Note that implicit in this analysis are the following assumptions: resources are fully employed all the time other-wise resources can be attracted into industry C at no oppor-tunity cost; costless adjustment, in the sense that the trans-fer of resources from other sectors to industry C is smooth and requires no extra expenditures; homogeneous factors of pro-duction; perfectly competitive markets; and unaltered levels of consumer expenditure. Changes in these assumptions would result in drastically different conclusions – see next chapter.

Tariffs have another effect which is not of particular relevance here but which needs to be mentioned. It was stressed earlier that tariffs reduce the level of imports by q_1q_2 plus q_3q_4. The previous cost of these imports was q_1AEq_2 plus q_3FBq_4 which had to be paid in foreign currency equivalent. Hence, these sums represent savings in foreign exchange and may, therefore, be of great significance for a country with a severe balance of payments constraint. They are, therefore, referred to as the balance of payments effects of a tariff.

Finally, it should be apparent that the extent of the dead-weight losses is determined by the slopes of SS and DD, i.e. by the price elasticities of H's supply and demand curves, given S_W. The more elastic these curves, the less the welfare losses due to tariff imposition.

To recap, tariffs, given the analysis conducted so far, have: (i) a consumption effect; (ii) a production effect; (iii) a revenue effect; (iv) a redistribution effect; and (v) an import effect. In short, tariffs benefit the producers and the government and penalise the consumer and the foreign pro-ducer – a tariff is equivalent to an excise duty on the con-sumer, the revenue from which is received by domestic pro-ducers with the residual accruing to the government.

Import Quota Restrictions

Analysing the welfare effects of import quota restrictions is also straightforward. Starting from the free trade position depicted in figure 8.1, an import quota of q_2q_3 can be effect-ively introduced only if the world price (P_W) diverges from the domestic price (P_W^t) by a percentage which results in that quota. In other words, the quota produces an implicit differ-ence between world and domestic prices that generates the specified quota. Once the domestic price rises to the level

that makes that quota restriction possible, the analysis
follows the same pattern as that of a tariff. Hence, in this
sense, tariffs and quotas are equivalent in their effects.

There is one basic difference though. With a tariff, the
area EDCF is a tariff revenue for the government, but what
happens to that area in a quota system depends on the assumptions made regarding the way in which the quota is administered
and the competitive nature of importers and exporters. If the
government decides to issue the quota itself, it will be able
to generate a revenue from this activity equal to area EDCF.
If the importers operate as a cartel to administer the quota
and face perfectly competitive W suppliers they can reap area
EDCF as excess profits. However, if W's exporters act as a
cartel facing perfectly competitive H importers, W will reap
that area as excess profits.

Of course, more complicated situations can be envisaged.
For example, what if both importers and exporters organise
themselves into cartels? It is then possible to envisage a
monopoly versus monopsony outcome where the relative strength
of the two countries determines what percentage of EDCF each
acquires. In short, quotas create problems with regard to the
area previously analysed as tariff revenue accruing to the
government.

Equivalence of Tariffs and Quotas

Given the qualification regarding the organisation and distribution of the quota, it was demonstrated that tariffs and
quotas are equivalent in their effects in that they produce
the same production, consumption, revenue, distribution and
import effects. However, that conclusion was reached by
assuming that: (i) the foreign supply was competitive; (ii)
there was perfect competition in domestic production; and
(iii) there was perfect competition among the quota holders
with one implication being that the full quota was used. It
is of interest to know what qualifications to that conclusion
need to be made as a result of relaxing some of these assumptions.

In order to answer this question meaningfully, consider
the case where S_W is not perfectly elastic. In figure 8.2 SS,
DD, S_W and S_W^t are defined as before. Note that S_W and S_W^t are
both upward sloping and the vertical distance between them
measures the ad valorem tariff (if the tariff were specific,
S_W and S_W^t would be parallel). $S + S_W^t$ is the total supply
curve facing H in the presence of tariffs.

Given tariff imposition, H's domestic price is P resulting in domestic production and consumption Oq_1 and Oq_2 respectively with q_1q_2 imports from W. The price in W now has to
be found since S_W is no longer perfectly elastic. To determine P_W drop a vertical line from the point where S_W^t crosses
the horizontal at P. The vertical distance between P and P_W

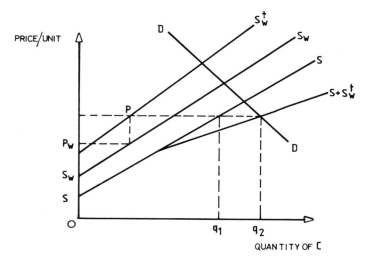

FIG. 8.2

as a proportion of P_W measures, by definition, the tariff rate.
Hence, this tariff rate results in imports of q_1q_2. Now, if
instead of a tariff an import quota of q_1q_2 is introduced, the
quota will result in the same divergence between domestic and
world prices. Therefore, corresponding to every import level
there will be some (implicit) tariff rate. Moreover, a tariff
will generate an import level which, set alternatively, as a
quota, would generate the same tariff rate. In short, the
tariff and quota alternatives are equivalent; more precisely
"an explicit tariff rate will produce an import level which,
if set <u>alternatively</u> as a quota, will produce an implicit tariff
equal to the explicit tariff (and, pairwise, that a quota will
produce an implicit tariff which, if set <u>alternatively</u> as an
explicit tariff will generate the same level of imports)"
(Bhagwati 1965, p. 248).

Now consider the situation where assumptions (i) and (iii)
are still valid but where the second assumption is replaced by
monopoly in domestic production. A monopolist who adopts a
profit-maximising behaviour will strive for equality of marginal cost (MC) and marginal revenue (MR). Hence the analysis
has to be adjusted to incorporate this dimension.

In figure 8.3a, DD, S_W and S_W^t are defined as before but
dCD is the demand facing the domestic monopolist; dCD is derived by subtracting S_W^t (the foreign supply in the presence of
tariffs) from DD (the total demand for commodity C). Hence, at

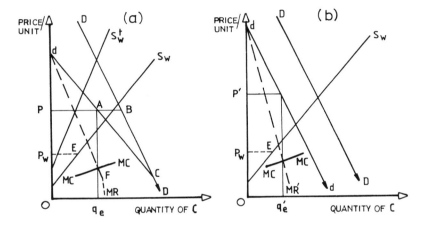

FIG. 8.3

d the demand for the domestic monopolist is equal to zero since S_W^t is equal DD. Also, at C the total demand is entirely available for the domestic monopolist since S_W^t is equal to zero. The diagram also includes the MR curve corresponding to dCD (recall that MR slopes twice as fast as dCD and that there is a kink at point F due to the differing slopes of the two portions of dCD — dC and CD) and the domestic monopolist's MC curve.

Equilibrium output (q_e) is determined at the intersection of MC and MR. This results in the domestic price P and imports equal to AB. The divergence between the domestic price and the foreign price (P_W) is ($P-P_W$)/OP_W. Note that $P_W E$ is equal to AB and is obtained by dropping a vertical line to S_W from

99

the point of intersection of PB and S_W^t.

If, instead of a tariff, H introduces a quota equal to AB, the demand curve facing the domestic monopolist will be DD minus AB − dd in figure 8.3b where S_W, DD and MC are exactly those of figure 8.3a. Hence, dd is parallel to DD.

dd has its own MR curve − MR'. Following the previous procedure, it follows that the domestic price is equal to P', the foreign price is still P_W (since the level of imports remains unaltered) and the divergence between the two is equal to $(P'-P_W)/OP_W$. Since the two portions of figure 8.3 are drawn to scale, it is clear that the divergence between the domestic and foreign prices created by the quota is higher than that due to the tariff. Hence, tariffs and quotas are no longer equivalent in their effects.

If this explanation is not entirely clear, it should become so when one realises that dd is steeper than dCD. Imagine a line to the left of DD (in figure 8.3a) and parallel to it passing through point A; that is dd (of figure 8.3b). Hence, MR' is steeper than MR and since MC is exactly the same in both cases, it follows that MR' intersects MC to the left of its intersection with MR, i.e. less output is produced as a result of the quota. Also, since the portion of this (imaginary) dd above A necessarily lies above dCD, it also follows that the domestic price resulting from the quota (P') is higher than P. Therefore, the quota generates a higher implicit tariff.

Finally, the non-equivalence of tariffs and quotas does not arise only when perfectly competitive production is replaced by monopoly in production; similar (but slightly qualified) conclusions can be reached with the assumptions of: (i) monopoly of quota holding in place of perfect competition among the quota holders; (ii) monopoly in quota holding and in domestic production; and (iii) monopoly in the supply of imports (see Bhagwati 1969, pp.254-61).

In concluding this section it should be emphasised that the question of equivalence (or lack of it) is not only of theoretical interest but is also of practical significance. For example, even if equivalence prevailed, a society might find a quota more acceptable than its equivalent tariff if the tariff proved to be very high, say about 100 per cent.

General Equilibrium Analysis

In preparation for the following chapter, it is important to generalise the analysis of tariffs to the country as a whole; so far the analysis has been confined to a single and insignificant industry. However, the assumption of constant t/t will be retained hence the following analysis is still applicable, but only to a 'small' country.

In chapter four, the free trade general equilibrium analysis was demonstrated in terms of a production possibility frontier (PPF) and a set of community indifference curves (CICs) – see figure 4.5. The PPF is depicted by HH in figure 8.4. When a tariff is imposed, given constant t/t (t_i4 in figure 8.4), the domestic price of the commodity in question (C) rises. Here P_i and C_i are the respective free trade production and consumption points with this country importing commodity C in exchange for exports of commodity F; the right angled triangle determined by P_i and C_i gives the level of trade.

Note that the total value of production is equal to O4 in terms of commodity C or O5 in terms of commodity F. This can be explained simply. The production of C and F, under free trade, is given by point P_i; Oc_1 of C and Of_1 of F. Given t/t t_i4, Oc_1 (= f_1P_i) of C can be exchanged for f_15 of F; alternatively Of_1 (= c_1P_i) of F can be exchanged for c_14 of C. Hence, O4 can be purchased by O5 and vice versa – i.e. t_i4 <u>is</u> a precise ratio.

The imposition of the tariff results in domestic price ratio t_i^t. This leads to expansion in the production of commodity C <u>and</u> contraction in the production of commodity F – since HH <u>is</u> the full employment PPF, the expansion of one industry must necessarily have a positive opportunity cost. Now, since the country <u>as a whole</u> continues to trade at the given t/t (t_i4), the <u>total post-tariff</u> value of production falls to O3 in terms of commodity C (P_i^t3 is parallel to t_i4). Hence, the tariff has a cost equal to 34 in terms of commodity C.

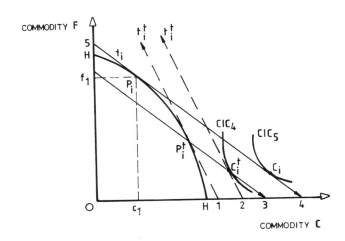

FIG. 8.4

What is the precise level of post-tariff consumption?
The answer is easily provided if it is recalled that the tariff
creates government revenue and it is assumed that this is returned to the consumer, for example in the form of a reduction in other taxes. Hence, consumers' income is in excess of
the domestic value of post-tariff income (Ol which is determined by t_i^t1). Therefore, the post-tariff consumption point
must be on P_i^t3; more precisely at the point on P_i^t3 where a CIC
is at a tangent to a line parallel to t_i^t1. In other words, it
must be an equilibrium consumption point with respect to the
domestic price ratio but must also lie on t/t parallel to t_i4
since the country as a whole is still trading at the given
world price ratio. Hence C_i^t is the post-tariff consumption
point and the distance 12 gives the tariff revenue in terms of
commodity C.

It should be emphasised that since points C_i and C_i^t lie
on parallel lines they must be on the society's income consumption curve. Moreover, since line t_i4 represents higher income
than line P_i^t3 (due to the tariff) it follows that as long as
both commodities C and F are normal goods (neither is inferior)
point C_i must lie to the NE of point C_i^t. Hence the tariff
results in a lower level of consumption of commodity C in comparison with the free trade position.

Finally, note that the post-tariff trade level given by
the right angled triangle formed by points P_i^t and C_i^t is lower
than that under free trade. Hence, the tariff reduces the
volume of trade; more specifically it results in lower imports
of commodity C.

In concluding this section, it should be stated that the
above analysis, given in general equilibrium terms, leaves intact the previous conclusions reached in terms of partial equilibrium analysis: (i) the domestic production of the imported
commodity rises; (ii) the domestic consumption of that commodity falls, provided it is not an inferior good; (iii) the
level of imports of that commodity falls; (iv) the tariff has
a revenue effect; and (v) the tariff has a welfare effect measured in terms of CIC_4 as against CIC_5 or distance 34 in terms
of commodity C. However, a new conclusion emerges: since
production of C increases while that of F falls (move from P_i
to P_i^t), the tariff has (vi) an income redistribution effect
such that the factor used intensively in the production of
commodity C is made better off and the factor used intensively
in the production of commodity F is made worse off. This
emerges clearly from the discussion in chapters 3, 6 and 7 so
there is no need to expand on it here.

Conclusion

The effects of tariff imposition discussed in this chapter are
entirely dependent on the crucial assumptions that the t/t
remain constant (the 'small' country assumption) and that tariff

imposition raises the domestic price of the commodity being protected. These assumptions will be carefully considered in chapter 9.

Chapter Nine

OPTIMUM TARIFFS AND RETALIATION

Introduction

In the previous chapter, the economic consequences of tariff
imposition were analysed under conditions of constant t/t.
However, in a world economy, the imports of one country are
the exports of another, so the imposition of a tariff on one
commodity by one country should be analysed in terms of the
markets in both countries.
    Figure 9.1a depicts the situation in the tariff imposing
country (H) while figure 9.1b shows that of the exporting
country – the rest of the world (W). Under free international
trade conditions, given the supply and demand functions facing
the two countries, this commodity (C) will be exported by W
and imported by H since the sufficiency price in H exceeds
that in W – see chapter 6. Suppose the free trade price
settles at P_i – recall that international trade equalises
commodity prices. H's imports (ab) will be equal to W's exports (a*b*). When H imposes a tariff rate of $P_H P_i / O P_i$ on C,
the domestic price of C rises to P_H leading to a fall in imports (from ab to cd). It should be obvious that W can supply
this new level of imports (cd = c*d* in W) only if the price
in W falls to P_W. Hence, the tariff has created a difference
between the relative prices in H and W; more precisely, W's
export price has fallen which is tantamount to stating that
the t/t have changed in favour of the tariff imposing country.
Hence, tariffs have a t/t effect. The purpose of this chapter
is to analyse the economic consequences of this aspect of
tariffs.

Tariffs and Offer Curves

Instead of proceeding in partial equilibrium terms, it is useful to use general equilibrium analysis to study the effects
of tariff imposition on the t/t. The analytical apparatus
needed is that developed in chapter 5. There, traded commodities were depicted by offer curves. In figure 9.2, OO and

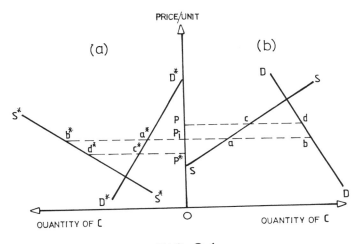

FIG. 9.1

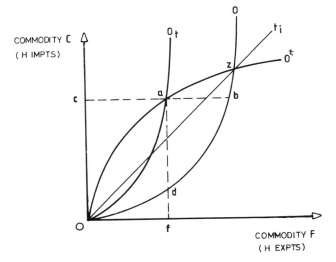

FIG. 9.2

$OO*$ are the respective free trade offer curves for H and W which result in equilibrium t/t given by t_i. The imposition of a tariff by H results in a new offer curve (O_t). This can be explained as follows. If the tariff is a tax on the imported commodity (C), H, prior to tariff imposition, exported Of in exchange for df of imports but now requires ad more imports as a result of the tariff imposition. Hence ad is the tariff revenue and ad/df is the tariff rate. If the tariff is a tax on exports, H, before the tariff, offered cb of exports in exchange for Oc of imports, but now offers only ca with ab being the tariff revenue and ab/ca the tariff rate. Therefore, irrespective of how the tariff is specified, its imposition produces an offer curve for H that lies between the original (tariff free) offer curve (OO) and the vertical axis - the difference between the two representing the tariff rate.

Similarly, a tariff by W will result in an offer curve O_t^* (not drawn) between $OO*$ and the horizontal axis. Moreover, if instead of tariffs subsidies (or income transfers) became the order of the day, the offer curves would move in the opposite direction.

Now, starting at the free trade point (z) with equilibrium t/t given by t_i, the introduction of a tariff by H results in a new equilibrium point (a). Hence, the new t/t are given by the slope of the vector (not drawn) joining O and a. The new t/t are steeper than the free trade t/t, i.e. the same quantity of F can be exchanged for more C, given the tariff-ridden situation. Hence, the t/t have changed in favour of H's exportables and against its importables. However, the move from z to point a clearly indicates a fall in imports - Oz > Oa. Hence, tariff imposition has mixed economic consequences: favourable t/t changes and unfavourable (welfare reducing) lower import levels. These conflicting influences require further consideration.

Figure 9.3 is similar to figure 9.2 but contains some extra information: it includes the TICs (TIC_5, TIC_6, TIC_7, TIC_3^*, TIC_4^* and TIC_5^*). The insertion of the TICs helps to clarify these conflicting considerations. A tariff that displaces OO to OO_t will improve H's welfare provided it is not so high as to result in an offer curve (not drawn) passing through point a. At point a, H stays on the same level of welfare as the free trade position (TIC_6). Any higher tariff will reduce H's welfare in comparison with the free trade situation. It is then quite apparent that a tariff which takes OO_t through point z_1 gives the highest possible level of welfare for H: at point z_1^*, H's TIC is at a tangent to W's offer curve indicating that a point to the NW of z_1 is not attainable. Note that at z_1 the t/t (measured by the vector Oz_1) have changed in favour of H but, at the same time, the level of trade has fallen.

The tariff that maximises the welfare of the country imposing it is referred to as the optimum tariff. Note that

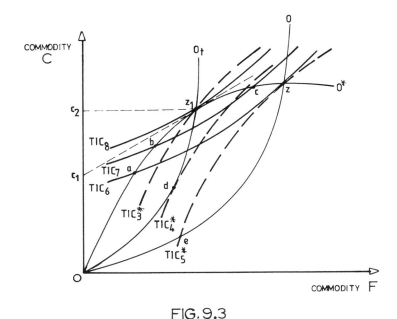

FIG. 9.3

if OO* were a straight line (i.e. H is a 'small' country facing
a 'large' world) any tariff by H would necessarily lower H's
welfare since the tariff here would simply reduce trade without affecting the t/t. Also note that the improvement in H's
welfare is simultaneously accompanied by a reduction in W's
welfare (W moves from TIC_5^* to TIC_3^*) hence the tariff is a
'beggar-my-neighbour' type of commercial practice.

Tariffs and Domestic Prices

In figure 9.1 it was clearly indicated that a tariff raises
the domestic price of the commodity under consideration. In
figures 9.2 and 9.3 it was demonstrated that the tariff improves H's t/t. It is important to know what happens to the
domestic price level in figures 9.2 and 9.3. This is simple
to establish if one recalls the analysis in chapter 5. In
figure 9.2 (or imagine point a of figure 9.2 to coincide with
point z_1 of figure 9.3, in which case the two figures are
identical) the free trade t/t are given by the slope of Ot_1,
while the tariff-ridden t/t are given by the slope of the vector
Oa (not drawn). The domestic price ratio is given by the slope
of the vector Ob (not drawn). This is due to the fact that
with a tariff rate of ab/ca, the domestic consumer pays yb
with the government capturing ab in tariff revenue, i.e. the
domestic and world prices differ by the tariff revenue. Since

Ob is flatter than Oz, it is then clear that the relative domestic price ratio has risen for the tariff-ridden commodity. However, this result does not always follow. In figure 9.4a the vector Oa is, again, steeper than the vector Oz but so too is Ob. Note that this result is entirely due to W's offer curve being backward-bending (inelastic) in the relevant section. Hence the normal conclusions apply only if the offer curves are elastic.

In figure 9.4b, $OO*$ and OO_t^* are W's respective free trade and tariff-ridden offer curves. OO' and OO are two possible offer curves. When H's offer curve is OO, tariff imposition by W improves W's t/t (vector Oz' is steeper than Oa') and raises the domestic price of the imported commodity (Ob' is steeper than Oz'). Hence, the normal conclusions apply. However, if H's offer curve is OO', it follows that both the international t/t and the domestic price ratio fall. Similar conclusions apply in the case of W being the tariff imposing country.

Optimum Tariff Formulae

The derivation of the optimum tariff (t_e) is straightforward. Recall that the general model utilised here is based on the premise of perfect competition in both commodity and factor markets. Hence H's domestic price (P) is equal to the world price (P*) plus the tariff: $P = P*(1 + t_e)$. In terms of

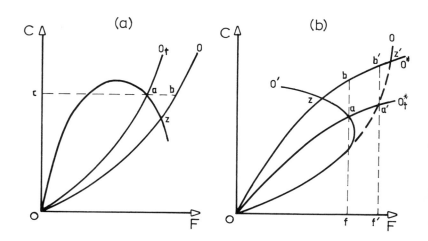

FIG. 9.4

figure 9.3, this can be expressed as:

$$\frac{c_2 z_1}{c_1 c_2} = \frac{c_2 z_1}{0 c_2} (1 + t_e),$$

since P can be approximated by the slope of the tangent to Z_1, given the way TICs were derived in chapter 5. This equation can be arranged to give:

$$t_e = \frac{0 c_2}{c_1 c_2} - 1. \tag{1}$$

Recall that $0 c_2 / c_1 c_2$ is a measure of the elasticity of the offer curve (ε_o) as derived in chapter 5. Hence:

$$t_e = \varepsilon_o - 1, \tag{2}$$

i.e. the optimum tariff is equal to the elasticity of the offer curve reduced by unity.

(2) is a basic formula from which various other formulae can be derived. For instance, $0 c_2 / c_1 c_2 - 1$ in (1) is equal to $0 c_1 / c_1 c_2$. Since $c_1 c_2 = 0 c_2$, it follows that this also equals:

$$0 c_1 / 0 c_2 - 0 c_1. \tag{3}$$

Dividing both the numerator and the denominator of (3) by $0 y_1$, one gets:

$$t_e = \frac{1}{(0 c_2 / 0 c_1) - 1}. \tag{4}$$

However, $0 c_2 / 0 c_1$ is the elasticity of the foreign demand curve (ε_{fd}) that can be derived from the offer curve (see Johnson, 1958). Hence,

$$t_e = \frac{1}{\varepsilon_{fd} - 1}. \tag{5}$$

This is the most widely used version of the optimum formulae. Its advantage is that it captures the essentials of the previous discussion: (i) if $\varepsilon_{fd} = \alpha$, $t = o$, i.e. a country facing a perfectly elastic foreign offer curve cannot gain from tariff imposition; and (ii) the more elastic the foreign offer curve (hence the more elastic the foreign elasticity of demand for exports) the lower the optimum tariff.

Tariff Retaliation

It became apparent from figure 9.3 that although free trade maximises world welfare, H, a single country, can do much better by imposing an optimum tariff, but H's improved welfare is clearly at the expense of W. Hence, it is not surprising that an individual nation should impose a tariff, provided, of course, it can do so with impunity. However, a closer look at figure 9.3 indicates that, given the tariff-ridden point z_1, W can impose an optimum tariff of its own and move to point d. This raises W's welfare and reduces H's. Moreover, given point d, H can impose another optimum tariff. Hence a process of optimum-tariff-cum-retaliation can be initiated and the final outcome will be determined by either the complete elimination of international trade or the reaching of a point where the intersection of the relevant offer curves has the

characteristic that each country's TIC is at a tangent to the
other country's offer curve (point Z* in figure 9.6).

When the final outcome, after several rounds of optimum
tariffs and retaliation, is reached with some international
trade still taking place, it will obviously be inside the area
bounded by the free trade offer curves OO and OO* (figure 9.3).
Within that area, it can be located in one of three possible
sections: (i) the area between OO* and TIC_6 (i.e. area az_1z);
(ii) the area between OO and TICs (i.e. area ez); (iii) the
remaining area – OO* up to a; a to z along TIC_6; z to e along
TIC_5^*; and eO along OO. If the final outcome is inside area
(i), H is better off and W worse off in relation to the free
trade situation, z. If it is inside area (ii), W is better off
while H is worse off in comparison with the tariff-free situation. However, if it is inside area (iii), then both H and W
are worse off. Therefore, it is not necessarily true that both
countries will be worse off as a result of mutual tariff imposition.

Before concluding this section it should be pointed out
that the optimum-tariff-cum-retaliation sequence may result in
a tariff cycle where an increase in one country's tariff leads
to an increase in the other's which in turn provokes a decrease
in the first country's tariff leading to a decrease in the
second's which again leads to an increase in the first country's
tariff, etc. (see Johnson 1958, pp. 42-44).

Retaliation : a Closer Look

The logic of retaliation based on figure 9.3 is quite straightforward: W is better off with retaliation (it reaches TIC_4^*)
than without it (TIC_3^*). However, is it still logical to retaliate if the optimum tariff position (z_1) results in the
position depicted in figure 9.5?

In figure 9.5, TIC_4^* passes inside the area bounded by
TIC_8 and TIC_3^* while in figure 9.3 it lies wholly to the SE of
TIC_8. In other words in figure 9.5 an outcome such as z* (on
the contract curve KK) will leave H on the same level of welfare as with the optimum tariff but will take W to TIC_5^* – a
position far superior to the one it could achieve by retaliation.

Note that a final outcome which takes both countries to a
point such as z* or along KK between z* and z** will require a
reduction in H's tariff simultaneously accompanied by a subsidy
(or income transfer) by W. This possibility is interesting
since it implies that W should strive to persuade H to reduce
its tariff in return for an income subsidy. In other words,
such an outcome necessitates some kind of 'international cooperation' (see El-Agraa 1979). Indeed, this analysis suggests
that, given the situation depicted by figure 9.5, retaliation
as a mere act will be undertaken only to reprimand H for having
introduced the tariff in the first place or to induce

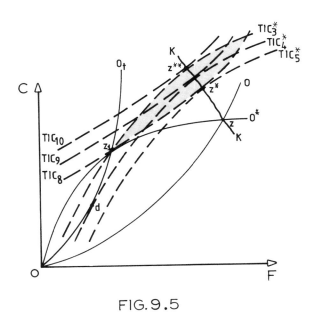

FIG.9.5

'international cooperation' from point d. The latter alternative not only results in a shaded area closer to z, the free
trade point but also communicates to H that W 'means business'
so that cooperation is undertaken from a point of relative
strength (El-Agraa 1979).

Moreover, there is another interesting possibility.
Suppose H is a very poor country which is large enough to
exert an influence on trade, e.g. India or China. When such a
country imposes a tariff, the world's attention is drawn to
its plight with the result that W assumes responsibility for
that country or concedes the point that it is entitled to a
welfare transfer in its favour, e.g. foreign aid. Hence, W

111

tells H that it will not issue a reprimand; instead it will grant aid provided the tariff is reduced. Indeed, this could be done in such a way that the final outcome is at z** with W remaining at TIC_3^* while H is allowed to reach a higher TIC than that obtainable with the optimum tariff (TIC_{10}). Therefore, such a possibility is far from abstract theory; it has a great intuitive practical appeal.

Finally, retaliation may be ruled out for the simple reason that the tariff-imposing country acts <u>unilaterally</u> while the international community is composed of many countries incapable of acting <u>in unison</u>. Hence, H can safely assume that the adoption of an optimum tariff need not necessarily induce retaliation by W.

Tariff Bargaining

International trade theorists used to pose the question: if countries harm themselves by imposing tariffs why do they not simply unilaterally reduce or eliminate their tariffs and be better off? (Johnson 1965). This is an interesting question because if it is legitimate it makes nonsense of certain rounds of tariff negotiation conducted under the auspices of GATT. In tariff negotiations, the two countries most concerned bargain for tariff reductions which, once agreed, are applied to all members of GATT - hence the principle of the most-favoured-nation clause. The essence of these tariff rounds is that countries bargain for tariff reductions: H will be willing to reduce or eliminate its tariff <u>provided</u> W is willing to do likewise.

It should be apparent from the earlier analysis that a country which stands to lose from tariff imposition must be one facing a perfectly elastic foreign offer curve. As was shown on purely economic grounds, such a country would be acting <u>irrationally</u>. Hence, the question becomes serious only if it is applicable to countries that have been adopting <u>rational</u> tariff decisions.

In figure 9.6, z is the free trade equilibrium point and z* depicts a tariff-cum-retaliation final (optimum) situation, i.e. when point z* is reached neither country stands to gain from further tariff imposition since each country's offer curve is at a tangent to the other's TIC. z* is therefore one of many points inside the area bounded by OO and OO* which depict a situation where <u>both</u> H and W have been imposing tariffs on each other. In other words, z* need not be an optimum point.

Starting from point z* it can be clearly seen that if H (W) adopts a <u>unilateral</u> tariff reduction it stands to lose since such action takes H (W) to a TIC to the SE (NW) of TIC (TIC*). However, a <u>joint</u> tariff reduction will result in the new offer curves intersecting <u>inside</u> the shaded area, hence moving <u>both</u> H and W to higher TICs. It can then be

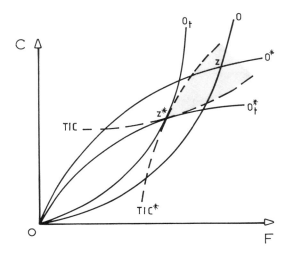

FIG. 9.6

categorically stated that, if countries have been imposing tariffs on each other's trade, unilateral tariff reduction is harmful to the country contemplating it while joint tariff reduction is welfare-improving for both (El-Agraa 1979 and 1981). Therefore, contrary to a claim by the late Professor Johnson (1965), this analysis provides an orthodox theoretical basis for 'tariff bargaining' - for an alternative framework see chapter 12.

Effective Protection

Throughout the analysis, it was observed that tariffs lead to expansion in domestic production of the protected industry, i.e. the tariff wall protects the domestic producer. However, in the real world, the production of a commodity may require the use of an 'intermediate' product which may also be imported and subject to a tariff of its own. The duty on the imported intermediate product is equivalent to a tax on production since it is tantamount to a vertical shift of SS in figure 8.1. The theoretical framework which takes these considerations into account is called the theory of tariff structures or effective protection and the rate of duty so calculated is referred to as the effective rate of protection (e).

e takes into account the fact that the 'nominal' tariff on an imported (finished) commodity does not by itself indicate the effective protection afforded to the relevant import-competing industry if that industry utilises inputs which are themselves subject to a tariff. The import-competing industry adds value to the imported input, and the effective protection of this 'value added' is the key indicator of how protection effects resource allocation

e tries to measure the percentage by which value added can increase over the free trade level as a result of a tariff structure. Denoting the <u>fixed</u> free trade price of a <u>final</u> commodity by p_j^*, a nominal tariff rate of t_j on its imports makes the domestic price $(1+t_j)p_j^*$. If the productive process uses an imported input i, with fixed world price p_i^* subject to its own tariff t_i, the domestic price of this input will be $(1+t_i)p_i^*$. Assuming that the quantity of this input required per unit of final output is fixed and denoting it by a_{ij}, then at free trade world prices the value added per unit of final output (v_j^*) is: $v_j^* = p_j^* - a_{ij}p_i^*$. The value added at domestic post-tariff prices (v_j), is equal to:
$$v_j = (1+t_j)p_j^* - a_{ij}(1+t_i)p_i^*.$$
Hence, by definition:
$$e_j = \frac{v_j - v_j^*}{v_j^*} = \frac{t_j p_j^* - t_i a_{ij} p_i^*}{p_j^* - a_{ij}p_i^*}.$$

Dividing both numerator and denominator by the world price of the final commodity p_j^*, and denoting the <u>share</u> of the imported input in a pound sterling's worth of final output at free trade prices by Θ_{ij}, i.e. $\Theta_{ij} = a_{ij}p_i^*/p_j^*$, the effective rate of protection afforded to the final commodity is:
$$e_j = \frac{t_j - \Theta_{ij}t_i}{1 - \Theta_{ij}}.$$

This is the key formula the implications of which can readily be summarised as follows:

(i) if $t_j = t_i$ then $e_i = t_i = t_j$, i.e. the 'nominal' and 'effective' rates are equal;

(ii) if $t_j > t_i$ then $e_j > t_j > t_i$;

(iii) if $t_j < t_i$ then $e_j < t_j < t_i$;

(iv) if $t_j < \Theta_{ij}t_i$ then $e_j < 0$; and

(v) if $t_j = 0$ then $e_j = -\Theta_{ij}t_i/(1-\Theta_{ij})$, i.e. it is negative.

These implications are equally valid when the number of imported inputs is equal to n since in that case:
$$e_j = \frac{t_j - \sum_{i=1}^{n}\Theta_{ij} i}{1 - \sum_{i=1}^{n}\Theta_{ij}}.$$

An interesting point to stress is that indicated by (iv) and (v) but particularly (v): if the nominal tariff on the final product is zero then any tariff on the imported input

that raises the domestic price of that input is a tax on it
and will therefore result in negative effective protection for
that commodity - i.e. the vertical shift of SS in figure 8.1,
despite the tariff on the finished product, results in a
domestic level of output short of Oq_1.

Conclusion

In this chapter the tariff analysis of the previous chapter
was extended to include the concepts of: (i) optimum tariff;
(ii) retaliation; and (iii) effective protection. Moreover,
the chapter introduced two new developments in this area: (iv)
international cooperation; and (v) tariff bargaining. In the
next chapter, the remaining areas regarding a rationale for
tariffs will be incorporated to conclude this section of the
book.

Chapter Ten

TARIFFS : SOME FURTHER ISSUES

Introduction

To conclude the discussion of the theory of tariffs (with the
exception of the preferential tariff arrangements tackled in
the following chapter), this chapter is devoted to a brief
analysis of various arguments which are usually advanced in
support of protection as a general policy stance. In a sense,
the discussion is about the non-arguments referred to in
chapter 8. Before embarking on this, however, the chapter
begins with a consideration of the tariff as a source of revenue.

Tariffs for Revenue

In some developing countries, where the tax system and structure is still at an early stage, governments tend to rely
heavily on tariffs as a source of revenue. This dependence
has some interesting implications. For instance, if the imported commodities are consumer goods, demand has to be fairly
inelastic (due to lack of domestic substitutes or simply because it is prestigious to buy 'foreign'), otherwise the tariff
may eliminate trade altogether and therefore deprive the government of its revenue. Also, such countries may have taxes
on exports which reduce their export sales and diminish their
foreign exchange earnings so creating balance of payments
bottlenecks and damaging any prospects of success for their
development plans since such plans tend to depend on imports
of the necessary capital equipment. Therefore, taxing foreign
trade for revenue purposes causes some complications.
    An interesting question is whether or not the optimum
tariff maximises tariff revenue. Consider figure 10.1 where
OO, OO_t, $O*$ and TICs are defined as before. Point z_1 depicts
the optimum tariff for country H. It was stated in the previous
chapter that the slope of c_1z measures the domestic price
ratio given the way TICs were derived in chapter 5. It was
also demonstrated in chapter 9 that the slope of the vector Oa

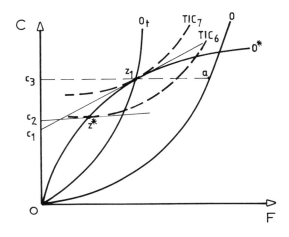

FIG. 10.1

(not drawn) measures the domestic price ratio. Hence Oa is parallel to c_1z. Now since z_1a is the tariff revenue in terms of commodity F and z_1a/c_3z_1 is the tariff rate and since c_1z_1 and Oa are parallel to each other, it follows that c_3c_1/Oc_1 is equal to c_3z_1/z_1a. Hence, the tariff revenue can be expressed in terms of commodity C as Oc_1. It is then clear that the optimum tariff results in tariff revenue Oc_1 while a tariff that results in O_t passing through point z^* will give domestic price c_2z^* and tariff revenue Oc_2. Therefore, the optimum tariff is not the maximum tariff revenue rate. Or, alternatively, in order to maximise tariff revenue a country will have to settle for a lower level of welfare: TIC_6 as against TIC_7.

Infant Industries

One of the most widely advanced justifications for protection is generally referred to as the 'infant industry' argument. If a country (H) believes it has a true comparative advantage in the production of a commodity, but history has enabled another country (W) to become established in its production and to capture the world market, that industry is known as an infant industry in H, and a tariff is often advocated to protect it while it develops. A classic example of an infant industry is 'textiles'. Textiles used to be a labour-intensive

117

industry; hence one would have expected the country with the
lower wage rate to have had a comparative advantage. However,
as the technology was not freely accessible (due to innovation
or patent rights) , the country with the technology produced
the commodity even though its wage rate was higher – the assumption is that no viable 'alternative' technology existed (a
cottage industry is not an alternative). The latter country,
therefore, initiated production but had only a superficial
comparative advantage.

The essence of this argument can easily be captured by
reference to figure 10.2 where AC and AC* are the respective
average cost curves for an industry in H and W. Note that AC
lies consistently below AC*, hence true cost advantage is with
H. However, W has the historical advantage of producing this
commodity and produces Oq_2 at an average cost of q_2b. H,
knowing that it has the true advantage, wishes to start production of this commodity but because W is already established,
H will have to capture the market gradually. Hence H commences
with an output such as Oq_1. This results in an average cost
of q_1a (which is in excess of q_2b), hence the argument that
this industry needs to be protected until it is able to mature,
i.e. at a production rate of Oq_2, H's average cost (q_2c) will
be less than W's (q_2b). Hence, an infant industry is necessarily able to grow and when maturity is reached protection can
be dispensed with.

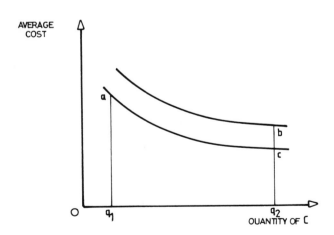

FIG. 10.2

This argument becomes much clearer when illustrated in general equilibrium terms. In figure 10.3, HH is H's PPF and CIC_1, CIC_2, CIC_3, etc. are its CICs. Under conditions of free international trade, production is at P_i and consumption at C_i. H is, therefore, importing commodity C in exchange for exports of commodity F, the volume of trade being determined by the right-angled triangle contained within P_i and C_i. Now, H introduces a tariff to protect its infant industry C. The tariff is usually assumed to be prohibitive but, of course, does not have to be so. However, following the usual convention, a prohibitive tariff is assumed. This takes both production and consumption to point z, hence H is at a lower level of welfare (CIC_1 as against CIC_3).

The aim of this protection is to enable the industry to reap the available internal economies and this is tantamount to displacing the PPF to HH' which could lie consistently outside HH, but, again following convention, this PPF is drawn without any expansion in commodity F. When the infant industry has grown, the country removes the tariff barrier and returns to free trade. The new t/t could be different but, following usual convention, they will be made equal to the initial t/t given by t_i (i.e. t_i' is parallel to t_i). This results in production at P_i' and consumption at C_i' with the volume of trade being determined by the right-angled triangle bounded by C_i' and P_i'. Note that the pattern of trade has been reversed since H now exports commodity C and imports commodity F. (The diagram

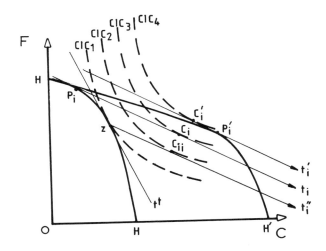

FIG.10.3

could be drawn so that the pattern of trade is not reversed but it should be apparent that that would be in direct contradiction of the basic premise for the existence of an infant industry.) Moreover, H is now at a higher level of welfare when compared with the initial tariff-free situation (CIC_4 as against CIC_3).

Before assessing this argument properly, it is vital to stress that the protection afforded to industry C may last for several years before the infant industry grows and reaches maturity. Hence, the loss of welfare incurred while the industry is growing (CIC_1 as against CIC_3) has to be multiplied by the time taken to reach maturity. Therefore, the final welfare improvement (CIC_4 as opposed to CIC_3) will have to more than compensate for the earlier loss. In other words, the essence of the infant industry argument is that the industry needs protection for a <u>specified</u> period of time and that the final benefits should be 'net' benefits.

Given these qualifications, and assuming that the calculations point to a 'net' benefit, it is still pertinent to ask whether or not the tariff is the best policy for achieving this end. To answer this question meaningfully two elements need to be included. Firstly, it should be clear from the analysis in chapter 9 that a subsidy to domestic production is superior to a tariff since a subsidy results in consumption at C_{ii} rather than at z (CIC_2 rather than CIC_1). Secondly, if a properly functioning investment market (capital market) existed, investors would be able to foresee the potential profitability of industry C in H and would, therefore, undertake the necessary long term investment. Hence, these two considerations render the argument null and void for any country which has sophisticated tax-revenue systems and capital markets. Advanced economies necessarily have both while some poor underdeveloped economies are most likely to lack both: capital markets simply do not exist and tariffs are the major source of government revenue. Moreover, such countries lack the necessary skills needed to operate such industries, hence an incentive to allow local labour to learn by doing is important. These considerations have, therefore, been influential in persuading international trade theorists that the infant industry argument is appropriate for such countries, <u>given</u> the provisos stated. That is why it has been conceded as the single exception to free trade.

In concluding this section it must be stressed that the infant industry argument is not, in a pure sense, an economic one; the argument is conceded for lack of the necessary prerequisites in such countries. The reader must therefore beware when such tariffs are proposed to support industries in advanced Western nations — see the Cambridge Economic Policy Group (Godley and Cripps 1976, Godley and May 1977 and Godley 1981) and El-Agraa's appraisal of their stance (El-Agraa 1982a, 1982b and 1983).

Tariffs and Domestic Distortions

Another interesting aspect of the theory of tariffs is whether protection is the best policy to adopt when a country is experiencing domestic distortions. Domestic distortions relate to a situation where there is a divergence between the commodity price ratio (P_X/P_Y) and the corresponding marginal rates of transformation $(MRTS_{F,C}^P$ and $MRS_{F,C}^C)$. This field has attracted a voluminous literature; however, the main issues were clarified by Hagen (1958), Bhagwati and Ramaswami (1969), Johnson (1965a), and Kemp and Negishi (1969).

It should be emphasised from the start that the issue regarding the use of tariffs in the presence of domestic distortions requires adequate answers to three questions. Firstly, is the tariff better than free trade? Secondly, is the tariff better than alternative forms of trade intervention? Finally, given a free choice, which is the optimal policy to adopt?

A simple framework exists for answering these questions. It was demonstrated in chapter 4 that an optimum situation requires equality of $MRTS_{F,C}^P$, $MRS_{F,C}^C$ and t_i, i.e.:

$$MRTS_{F,C}^P = MRS_{F,C}^C = t_i = P_C/P_F = td.$$

In the voluminous literature on this subject, t_i is referred to as the foreign rate of transformation (FRT), while $MRTS_{F,C}^P$ and $MRS_{F,C}^C$ are referred to respectively as the domestic rate of transformation in production (DRT) and the domestic rate of transformation in consumption (DRS). Now, if H has a monopoly power in international trade, the free trade situation will result in: DRS = DRT $\neq$ FRT. When H adopts an optimum tariff this leads to: DRS = DRT = FRT. Hence, equality is restored. However, if H levies a tax on the exportable commodity or subsidises the domestic production of the importable good this will result in: DRS $\neq$ DRT = FRT. Hence, the optimum tariff policy is superior to a tax-cum-subsidy policy. Now, in the presence of domestic distortions the free trade situation is characterised by: DRS = FRS $\neq$ DRT. The adoption of an appropriate tariff will lead to DRS $\neq$ FRS = DRT while an appropriate tax-cum-subsidy on domestic production will result in DRS = FRT = DRT. Therefore, in the presence of domestic distortions, a tariff policy is necessarily inferior to a tax-cum-subsidy policy. These conclusions are equally valid in the case of trade subsidies versus domestic tax-cum-subsidy policies. It is, therefore, not surprising when Bhagwati (1969b, p.296) states that, in the presence of domestic distortions, three propositions emerge: (i) a tariff is not necessarily superior to free trade; (ii) a tariff is not necessarily superior to an export (or import) subsidy; and (iii) the attainment of maximum welfare, generally requires a tax-cum-subsidy on domestic production.

These arguments can easily be illustrated in geometrical terms. However, not all the possible cases need to be discussed since two such illustrations should be sufficient to establish the general principles involved.

1. Domestic distortions in commodity markets.

The infant industry argument discussed earlier is based on the assumption that the industry is subject to internal economies. The prevalence of external economies or diseconomies, on the other hand, may lead to a divergence between social and private costs and benefits. Therefore, the question to be answered here is: can tariffs be used to correct such divergences and are they the best policy for doing so?

Consider an example of external diseconomies: an industry (commodity F) which is polluting the environment without being taxed for doing so. This means that private costs are below social costs of production. Hence, the relevant domestic price ratio (t_d) will not truly reflect the marginal opportunity cost of production. In figure 10.4, HH is a PPF reflecting the social opportunity costs of commodities C and F. The existence of external diseconomies in the production of commodity F results in the relative domestic price ratio indicated by t_d, with production and consumption at P_d - note that t_d <u>intersects</u> HH due to the lack of optimality created by the diseconomies. The international t/t are given by t_i indicating a less favourable international price for commodity C, i.e. H has a comparative advantage in commodity F, <u>given external diseconomies.</u> Under conditions of free trade, H will specialise in commodity F,

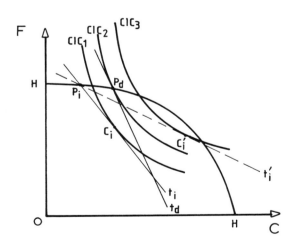

FIG. 10.4

producing at P_i and consuming at C_i. Hence, <u>in this example</u>, free international trade takes H to a lower $\overline{CIC}$ $(\overline{CIC_1})$. This is because the existence of external diseconomies has allowed H to specialise in the wrong commodity in the presence of unimpeded trade. However, deterioration in welfare is not the only possible outcome. If the international t/t is that given by $t_i^!$, H will consume at $C_i^!$ and is, therefore, better off with free trade.

Now suppose protection is adopted as a corrective measure. It should be obvious, from the general argument given at the beginning of this section, that tariffs will not result in the restoration of optimality. Hence, it does not matter whether the free trade situation leaves H better or worse off since a policy of tax-cum-subsidy will produce a better outcome than protection via a tariff – a tax-cum-subsidy will result in the relevant t/t being at a tangent to both the PPF (HH) and the relevant CIC. In other words, prohibitive protection will lead H back to P_d for both production and consumption while a tax-cum-subsidy will result in production along HH at the point where the relevant t_i (parallel to t_i in figure 10.4) is at a tangent to HH, and consumption somewhere to the NE of CIC_3 outside HH.

2. Domestic distortions in factor markets.

Another argument usually put forward in justification of protection is based on the existence of distortions in factor markets. This essentially means that a homogeneous factor of production is not being rewarded at the same rate in both sectors of the economy. This has the consequence that factors of production are not allocated in the most efficient way and therefore the PPF, reflecting this type of distortion, will be inside that derived on the assumption of optimum allocation – see chapter 3.

In figure 10.5, the solid HH curve reflects the true PPF for country H – that obtained with optimal allocation of resources. The broken HH curve reflects distortion in the factor market. A prohibitive protectionist position with domestic terms of trade given by t_d results in production and consumption at point P_d. Following the analysis of the previous case of distortion, it can be demonstrated that free trade may leave H better or worse off in comparison with point P_d. Hence, there is no need to complicate the diagram by illustrating that point.

Figure 10.5 depicts a situation with distortion in a factor employed in industry C. The international t/t, given by t_i, show a position that can be reached if commodity C receives a production subsidy; the subsidy takes H to the distorted PPF with production at $P_i^!$ and consumption at $C_i^!$. However, a tax-cum-subsidy on the distorted factor will restore the ideal PPF (the solid HH curve) leading to P_i and C_i as the

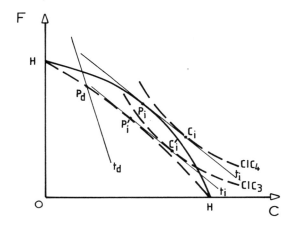

FIG. 10.5

respective production and consumption points (CIC_4 as against CIC_3).

Therefore the conclusion of this section is that a distortion must be corrected at its source. If the distortion relates to a commodity, a tax-cum-subsidy on that commodity results in the ideal situation. If the distortion relates to a factor, a tax-cum-subsidy on that factor is ideal. A tariff policy may or may not improve the distorted situation, but it must result in a sub-optimal outcome.

Conclusion

In concluding this chapter, it is useful to consider, very briefly, some other new developments in tariff theory. These developments (apart from those discussed in chapter 8) are concerned with three areas generally ignored in traditional analysis: (i) tariff seeking or tariff making; (ii) tariff evasion or smuggling; and (iii) revenue seeking. Tariff seeking analyses the situation where tariffs are imposed for protective, distributional or similar purposes, those who stand to benefit from them lobbying vigorously for the imposition of the tariff – see Cheh (1974), Brock and Magee (1978) and Findlay and Wellisz (1979). Tariff evasion is concerned with the notion that when tariffs prevail incentives are provided for attempts to evade them, e.g. smuggling or equivalent

measures — see Bhagwati (1964 and 1967), Johnson (1972),
Bhagwati and Hansen (1973), Bhagwati and Srinivasan (1973),
Bhagwati (1974), Sheikh (1974), Ray (1978) and Falvey (1978).
Finally, tariff seeking is concerned with the idea that if
tariffs create revenue, interested parties may lobby for a
share of that revenue — see Krueger (1974) and Bhagwati and
Srinivasan (1980).

At this level of exposition, it is unwise to embark on a
comprehensive analysis of these considerations. However, some
aspects of tariff seeking were included in the discussion of
the Stolper-Samuelson theorem (chapters 3 and 7) and some other
new developments are dealt with in chapter 11. The rest of
this chapter is, therefore, devoted to a discussion of some
aspects of revenue seeking.

The analysis so far has assumed that tariff revenue is
returned to the consumers as a lump-sum to be disposed of in
such a way that marginal valuations remain undisturbed. This,
of course, rules out the possibility of revenue seeking : "the
expenditure of real resources in the activity of getting a
share of the revenues resulting from tariff imposition"
(Bhagwati and Srinivasan, 1980, p. 1070). To overcome this
hurdle, it is assumed that lobbies exist and use <u>real</u> resources
in attempting to acquire a share of the tariff revenue.

In figure 10.6a, HH is the PPF for a 'small' country. The
imposition of a non-prohibitive tariff by H results in production and consumption, respectively, at P_2 and C_1, given a lump-
sum disposition of the tariff revenue. P_3 is the free trade
production point and DE is the tariff revenue expressed in
terms of commodity C. Now, revenue seeking implies that a
certain proportion of the factors of production (K and L) is
devoted to the lobbying activity (k + 1). Assuming perfect
competition in this lobby, the ratio k/1 employed here is determined according to the cost minimising conditions given in
chapter 3, on the understanding that a PF exists for this
activity: k/1 depends on w/π.

With incomplete specialisation in production, the tariff-
inclusive commodity price ratio is determined by the slope of
C_1D or C_2E. This in turn determines the factor price ratio w/π.
Since both commodity and factor prices are constant (the 'small'
country assumption), w/π determines the k/1 ratio employed in
the revenue seeking activity. Assuming that <u>all</u> tariff revenue
is available for seeking, it follows that the total quantity of
K and L employed in this activity is determined by DE.

Of course, the use of K and L in this activity diminishes
the amount of real resources available for the production of
commodities C and F. Moreover, given fixed commodity and
factor prices, domestic consumption of commodities C and F is
determined by domestic expenditure, which is identical to
national income at factor cost (the slope of C_1D), since
"domestic expenditure must equal domestic income in the revenue-
seeking equilibrium, and the latter is nothing but the value

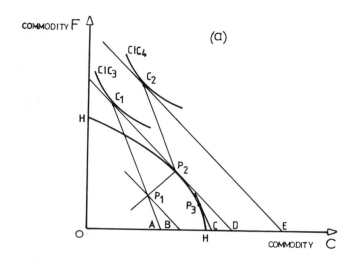

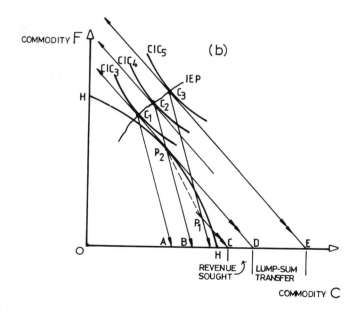

FIG. 10.6

of factors used in goods production plus the value of factors
diverted to revenue-seeking, which adds up to the value of all
factors at w and [π] associated with [P_2] and hence to national
income at factor cost at [P_2]" (Bhagwati and Srinivasan 1980,
p.1074).

It follows that consumption is determined by the equality
of the domestic commodity price ratio and the slope of a CIC.
Hence, consumption is at C_1. Production must lie along the
international t/t going through C_1, the precise position being
determined by the intersection of that line with the locus of
equilibria between production points and the domestic commodity
price ratio - the generalised Rybczynski line (see chapter 7).
This gives point P_1 as the new equilibrium production point.
It should be stressed that point P_1 must necessarily lie inside
HH since real resources are being diverted away from the production of commodities C and F.

Figure 10.6a demonstrates six interesting points: (i) the
new level of imports of the protected industry F may exceed or
fall short of the initial level since $C_1 P_1 \gtreqless C_2 P_2$; (ii) the new
level of tariff revenue (BD) may exceed or fall short of the
initial level since BD $\gtreqless$ DE; (iii) as long as P_1 lies along
C,A between C_1 and A (not at either point given the assumptions
made), the cost of the lobbying activity is independent of
changes in the k/l ratio employed in the lobby; (iv) if the
tariff imposition is to increase the production of commodity F,
tariff seeking may frustrate this objective since point P_1 may
lie to the SW of P_3; (v) a particular expansion target in the
production of commodity F, given tariff seeking, may require
a lower or higher tariff rate than in the absence of tariff
seeking; and (vi) contrary to the position depicted in
figure 10.6a, tariff seeking (as against no tariff seeking)
may improve the nation's welfare - see figure 10.6b where the
final consumption point is C_3 due to the assumption that part
of the tariff revenue (DE) is given as a lump-sum transfer
leaving only CD for tariff seeking and the fact that the generalised Rybczynski line ($P_1 P_2$) is flatter than the international t/t with IEP as the income expansion path.

Although this is an interesting new development, the
reader should be aware that there is nothing novel about it.
After all, "lobbies exist, and utilise real resources for the
pursuit of a share in the revenues that are disbursed by the
state, (Bhagwati and Srinivasan 1980, p. 1070), i.e. this
analysis applies to all equivalent taxes, for example, excise
duties on cigarettes.

Chapter Eleven

THEORY OF ECONOMIC INTEGRATION

Introduction

'International economic integration' is one aspect of 'international economics' which has been growing in importance in
the past two decades or so. The term itself has a rather
short history; indeed, Machlup (1977) was unable to find a
single instance of its use prior to 1942. Since then the term
has been used at various times to refer to practically any
area of international economic relations. By 1950, however,
the term had been given a specific definition by economists
specialising in international trade to denote a state of
affairs or a process which involves the amalgamation of separate economies into larger regions, and it is in this more
limited sense that the term is used today. More specifically,
international economic integration is concerned with the discriminatory removal of all trade impediments between the participating nations and with the establishment of certain elements of cooperation and coordination between them. The latter
depends entirely on the actual form that integration takes.
Different forms of international integration can be envisaged
and some have actually been implemented:
     (i) free trade areas where the member nations remove all
trade impediments among themselves but retain their freedom
with regard to the determination of their policies vis-a-vis
the outside world (the non-participants), for example, the
European Free Trade Association (EFTA), the Latin American Free
Trade Area (LAFTA), etc;
     (ii) customs unions which are very similar to free trade
areas except that member nations must conduct and pursue common
external commercial relations, for instance, they must adopt
common external tariffs on imports from the non-participants
as is the case in the European Community (EC); the EC is in
this particular sense a customs union, but it is more than that;
     (iii) common markets which are customs unions that also
allow for free factor mobility across national member frontiers,
i.e. capital, labour, enterprise should move unhindered

between the participating countries, for example, the East
African Community (EAC), the EC (but again it is more complex),
etc;

(iv) complete economic unions which are common markets
that ask for complete unification of monetary and fiscal
policies, i.e. a central authority is introduced to exercise
control over these matters so that existing member nations
effectively become regions of one nation;

(v) complete political integration where the participants
become literally one nation, i.e. the central authority needed
in (iv) not only controls monetary and fiscal policies but is
also responsible to a central parliament with the sovereignty
of a nation's government.

It should be stressed that each of these forms of economic
integration can be introduced in its own right: they should not
be confused with stages in a process which eventually leads to
complete political integration. It should also be noted that
within each scheme there may be sectoral integration, as distinct from general across-the-board integration, in particular
areas of the economy, for example in agriculture as is the case
in the EC - hence the Common Agricultural Policy (CAP). Of
course, sectoral integration can be introduced as an aim in
itself as was the case in the European Coal and Steel Community
(ECSC), but sectoral integration is a form of 'cooperation'
since it is not consistent with the accepted definition of
international economic integration.

It should be pointed out that international economic integration can be positive or negative. The term 'negative integration' was coined by Tinbergen (1954) to refer to the removal of impediments on trade between the participating nations
or to the elimination of any restrictions on the process of
trade liberalisation. The term 'positive integration' relates
to the modification of existing instruments and institutions
and, more importantly, to the creation of new ones so as to
enable the market of the integrated area to function properly
and effectively and also to promote other broader policy aims
of the union. Hence, at the risk of oversimplification, it can
be stated that sectoral integration and free trade areas are
forms of international economic integration which require only
'negative integration', while the remaining types require
'positive integration' since, as a minimum, they all require
the positive act of adopting common external relations. However, in reality, this distinction is unfair since practically
all existing types of international economic integration have
found it necessary to introduce some elements of 'positive integration'.

The Gains from Integration

In reality, almost all existing cases of economic integration
were either proposed or formed for political reasons even

though the arguments popularly put forward in their favour were expressed in terms of possible economic gains. However, no matter what the motives for economic integration are, it is still necessary to analyse the economic implications of such geographically discriminatory groupings.

At the customs union (and free trade area) level, the possible sources of economic gain can be attributed to

(i) enhanced efficiency in production made possible by increased specialisation in accordance with the law of comparative advantage;

(ii) increased production levels due to better exploitation of economies of scale made possible by the increased size of the market;

(iii) an improved international bargaining position, made possible by the larger size, leading to better terms of trade;

(iv) enforced changes in economic efficiency brought about by enhanced competition; and

(v) changes affecting both the amount and quality of the factors of production due to technological advances.

If the level of economic integration is to proceed beyond the customs union level, to the economic union level, then further sources of gain become possible due to

(vi) factor mobility across the borders of member nations;

(vii) the coordination of monetary and fiscal policies; and

(viii) the goals of near full employment, higher rates of economic growth and better income distribution becoming unified targets.

Let us now discuss these considerations in some detail.

The Customs Union Aspects

1. The basic concepts.

Before the theory of second-best was developed (Meade 1955 and Lipsey and Lancaster 1956-57) it used to be the accepted tradition that customs union formation should be encouraged. The rationale for this was that since free trade maximised world welfare and since customs union formation was a move towards free trade, customs unions increased welfare even though they did not maximise it. This rationale certainly lies behind the guidelines of the GATT articles which permit the formation of customs unions and free trade areas as the special exceptions to the rules against international discrimination.

Viner (1950) challenged this proposition by stressing the point that customs union formation is by no means equivalent to a move towards free trade since it amounts to free trade between the members and protection vis-a-vis the outside world. This combination of free trade and protectionism could result in 'trade creation' and/or 'trade diversion'. Trade creation is the replacement of expensive domestic production by cheaper imports from a partner and trade diversion is the replacement

of <u>cheaper initial imports</u> from the outside world by <u>more</u>
<u>expensive imports</u> from a partner. Viner stressed the point
that trade creation is beneficial since it does not affect the
rest of the world while trade diversion is harmful and it is
therefore the relative strength of these two effects which determines whether or not customs union formation should be advocated. It is therefore important to understand the implications of these concepts.

Assuming perfect competition in both the commodity and
factor markets, automatic full employment of all resources,
costless adjustment procedures, perfect factor mobility
nationally but perfect immobility across national boundaries,
prices determined by cost, three countries H (the home country),
P (the potential customs union partner) and W (the outside
world), plus all the traditional assumptions employed in tariff
theory, we can use a simple diagram to illustrate these two
concepts.

In figure 11.1, S_W is W's perfectly elastic tariff free
supply curve for this commodity; S_H is H's supply curve while
S_{H+P} is the joint H and P tariff free supply curve. With a
non-discriminatory tariff imposition by H of AD (T_H), the
effective supply curve facing H is BREFQT, i.e. its own supply
curve up to E and W's, subject to the tariff $[S_W (1 + t_H)]$,
after that. The domestic price is therefore OD which gives
domestic production of Oq_2, domestic consumption of Oq_3 and
imports of q_2q_3. H pays q_2LMq_3 for these imports while the
domestic consumer pays q_2EFq_3 with the difference (LEFM) being
the tariff revenue which accrues to the H government. This
government revenue can be viewed as a transfer from the consumers to the government with the implication that when the
government spends it, the marginal valuation of that expenditure should be exactly equal to its valuation by the private
consumers so that no distortions should occur.

If H and W form a customs union, the free trade position
will be restored so that Oq_5 will be consumed in H and this
amount will be imported from W. Hence free trade is obviously
the ideal situation. But if H and P form a customs union, the
tariff imposition will still apply to W while it is removed
from P. The effective supply curve in this case is BRGQT. The
price falls to OC resulting in a fall in domestic production
to Oq_1, an increase in consumption to Oq_4 and an increase in
imports to q_1q_4. These imports now come from P.

The welfare implications of these changes can be examined
by employing the concepts of consumers' and producers' surpluses. As a result of increased consumption, consumers' surplus rises by CDFG. Part of this (CDEJ) is a fall in producers' surplus due to the decline in domestic production and
another part (IEFH) is a portion of the tariff revenue now
transferred back to the consumer subject to the same condition
of equal marginal valuation. This leaves the triangles JEI
and HFG as gains from customs union formation. However,

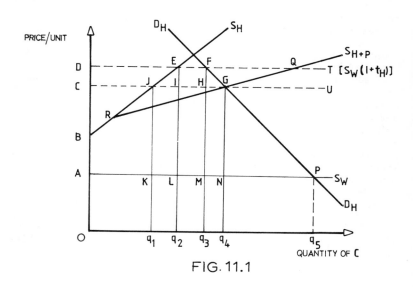

FIG. 11.1

before we conclude whether or not these triangles represent <u>net</u> gains we need to consider the overall effects more carefully.

The fall in domestic production from Oq_2 to Oq_1 leads to increased imports of q_1q_2. These cost q_1JIq_2 to import from P while they originally cost q_1JEq_2 to produce domestically. (Note that these resources are supposed to be employed elsewhere in the economy without any adjustment costs or redundancies.) There is therefore a saving of JEI. The increase in consumption from Oq_3 to Oq_4 leads to new imports of q_3q_4 which cost q_3HGq_4 to import from P. These give a welfare satisfaction to the consumers equal to q_3FGq_4. There is therefore an increase in satisfaction of HFG. However, the <u>initial</u> imports of q_2q_3 cost the country q_2LMq_3 but these imports now come from P costing q_2IHq_3. Therefore these imports lead to a loss equal to the loss in government revenue of LIHM (IEFH being a retransfer). It follows that the triangle gains (JEI + HFG) have to be compared with the loss of tariff revenue (LIHM) before a definite conclusion can be made regarding whether the net effect of customs union formation has been one of gain or loss.

It should be apparent that q_2q_3 represents, in terms of our definition, trade diversion, and q_1q_2 + q_3q_4 represent trade creation, or alternatively that areas JEI plus HFG are trade creation (benefits) while area LIHM is trade diversion (loss). (The reader should note that I am using Johnson's 1974 definition so as to avoid the unnecessary literature relating

132

to a trade-diverting welfare-improving customs union promoted
by Lipsey 1960, Gehrels 1956-57 and Bhagwati 1971 - see
El-Agraa and Jones 1981, chapter 2.) It is then obvious that
trade creation is economically desirable while trade diversion
is undesirable. Hence Viner's conclusion that it is the
relative strength of these two effects which should determine
whether or not customs union formation is beneficial or harmful.

The reader should note that if the initial price is that
given by the intersection of D_H and S_H (due to a higher tariff
rate), the customs union would result in pure trade creation
since the tariff rate is prohibitive. If the price is
initially OC (due to a lower tariff rate), then customs union
formation would result in pure trade diversion. It should
also be apparent that the size of the gains and losses depends
on the price elasticities of S_H, and S_{H+P} and D_H and on the
divergence between S_W and S_{H+P}, i.e. cost differences.

2. The Cooper/Massell criticism.

Viner's conclusion was challenged by Cooper and Massell (1965a).
They suggested that the reduction in price from OD to OC
should be considered in two stages: firstly, reduce the tariff
level indiscriminately (i.e. for both W and P) to AC which
gives the same union price and production, consumption and
import changes; secondly, introduce the customs union starting
from the new price OC. The effect of these two steps is
that the gains from trade creation (JEI + HFG) still accrue
while the losses from trade diversion (LIHM) no longer apply
since the new effective supply curve facing H is BJGU which
ensures that imports continue to come from W at the cost of
q_2LMq_3. In addition, the new imports due to trade creation
(q_1q_2 + q_3q_4) now cost less leading to a further gain of AJIL
plus MHGN. Cooper and Massell then conclude that <u>a policy of
unilateral tariff reduction is superior to customs union formation.</u>

3. Further contributions.

Following the Cooper/Massell criticism have come two independent but somewhat similar contributions to the theory of customs
unions. The first development is by Cooper and Massell (1965b)
themselves, the essence of which is that two countries acting
together can do better than each acting in isolation. The
second is by Johnson (1965) which is a private plus social
costs and benefits analysis expressed in political economy
terms. Both contributions utilise a 'public good' argument
with Cooper and Massell's expressed in practical terms and
Johnson's in theoretical terms. However, since the Johnson
approach is expressed in familiar terms this section is devoted
to it - space limitations do not permit a consideration of both.

Johnson's method is based on four major assumptions:
(i) governments use tariffs to achieve certain non-economic (political, etc.) objectives;
(ii) actions taken by governments are aimed at offsetting differences between private and social costs - they are, therefore, rational efforts;
(iii) government policy is a rational response to the demands of the electorate;
(iv) countries have a preference for industrial production. In addition to these assumptions, Johnson makes a distinction between private and public consumption goods, real income (utility enjoyed from both private and public consumption, where consumption is the sum of planned consumption expenditure and planned investment expenditure) and real product (defined as total production of privately appropriable goods and services).

These assumptions have important implications. Firstly, competition among political parties will make the government adopt policies that will tend to maximise consumer satisfaction from both 'private' and 'collective' consumption goods. Satisfaction is obviously maximised when the rate of satisfaction per unit of resources is the same in both types of consumption goods. Secondly, 'collective preference' for industrial production implies that consumers are willing to expand industrial production (and industrial employment) beyond what it would be under free international trade.

Tariffs are the main source of financing this policy simply because GATT regulations rule out the use of export subsidies and domestic political considerations make tariffs, rather than the more efficient production subsidies, the usual instruments of protection.

Protection will be carried to the point where the value of the marginal utility derived from collective consumption of domestic and industrial activity is just equal to the marginal excess private cost of protected industrial production. The marginal excess cost of protected industrial production consists of two parts: the marginal production cost and the marginal private consumption cost. The marginal production cost is equal to the proportion by which domestic cost exceeds world market cost. In a very simple model this is equal to the tariff rate. The marginal private consumption cost is equal to the loss of consumer surplus due to the fall in consumption brought about by the tariff rate which is necessary to induce the marginal unit of domestic production. This depends on the tariff rate and the price elasticities of supply and demand.

In equilibrium, the proportional marginal excess private cost of protected production measures the marginal 'degree of preference' for industrial production. This is illustrated in figure 11.2 where: S_W is the world supply curve at world market prices; D_H is the constant-utility demand curve (at

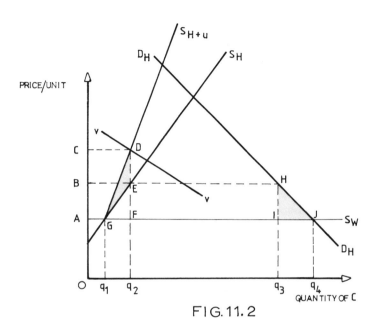

FIG. 11. 2

free trade private utility level); S_H is the domestic supply
curve; S_{H+u} is the marginal private cost curve of protected
industrial production, including the excess private consumption
cost [FE is the first component of marginal excess cost — determined by the excess marginal cost of domestic production in
relation to the free trade situation due to the tariff imposition (AB) — and the area GEF (= IHJ) is the second component
which is the dead loss in consumer surplus due to the tariff
imposition]; the height of vv above S_W represents the marginal
value of industrial production in collective consumption and
vv represents the preference for industrial production which
is assumed to yield a diminishing marginal rate of satisfaction.

135

The maximisation of <u>real</u> income is achieved at the intersection of vv with S_{H+u} requiring the use of tariff rate AB/OA to increase industrial production from Oq_1 to Oq_2 and involving the marginal degree of preference for industrial production v.

Note that the higher the value of v, the higher the tariff rate, and that the degree of protection will tend to vary inversely with the ability to compete with foreign industrial producers.

It is also important to note that, in equilibrium, the government is maximising real income, not real product: maximisation of real income makes it necessary to sacrifice real product in order to gratify the preference for collective consumption of industrial production.

Note also that this analysis is not confined to net importing countries. It is equally applicable to net exporters, but lack of space prevents such elaboration.

The above model helps to explain the significance of Johnson's assumptions. It does not, however, throw any light on the customs union issue; to make the model useful for this purpose it is necessary to alter some of the assumptions. Let us assume that industrial production is not one aggregate but a variety of products in which countries have varying degrees of comparative advantage; that countries differ in their overall comparative advantage in industry as compared with non-industrial production; that no country has monopoly/monopsony power (conditions for optimum tariffs do not exist); and that no export subsidies are allowed (GATT).

The variety of industrial production allows countries to be both importers and exporters of industrial products. This, in combination with the 'preference for industrial production', will motivate each country to practise some degree of protection.

Given the third assumption, a country can gratify its preference for industrial production only by protecting the domestic producers of the commodities it imports (import-competing industries). Hence the condition for equilibrium remains the same: $vv = S_{H+u}$. The condition must now be reckoned differently, however: S_{H+u} is slightly different because, firstly, the protection of import-competing industries will reduce exports of both industrial and non-industrial products (for balance of payments purposes). Hence, in order to increase total industrial production by one unit it will be necessary to increase protected industrial production by more than one unit so as to compensate for the induced loss of industrial exports. Secondly, the protection of import-competing industries reduces industrial exports by raising their production costs (due to perfect factor mobility). The stronger this effect, <u>ceteris paribus</u>, the higher the marginal excess cost of industrial production. This marginal excess cost will be greater, the larger the industrial sector compared with the non-industrial sector and the larger the protected industrial sector relative to the exporting industrial sector.

If the world consists of two countries, one must be a net exporter and the other necessarily a net importer of industrial products and the balance of payments is settled in terms of the non-industrial sector. Hence both countries can expand industrial production at the expense of the non-industrial sector. Therefore for each country the prospective gain from reciprocal tariff reduction must lie in the expansion of exports of industrial products. The reduction of a country's own tariff rate is therefore a source of loss which can only be compensated for by a reduction of the other country's tariff rate (for an alternative, orthodox, explanation see chapter 9 and El-Agraa 1979b and 1981).

What if there are more than two countries? If reciprocal tariff reductions are arrived at on a 'most-favoured nation' basis, the reduction of a country's tariff rate will increase imports from all the other countries. If the reduction is, however, discriminatory (starting from a position of non-discrimination), there are two advantages: firstly, a country can offer its partner an increase in exports of industrial products without any loss of its own industrial production by diverting imports from third countries (trade diversion); secondly, when trade diversion is exhausted any increase in partner industrial exports to this country is exactly equal to the reduction in industrial production in the same country (trade creation), hence eliminating the gain to third countries.

Therefore, discriminatory reciprocal tariff reduction costs each partner country less, in terms of the reduction in domestic industrial production (if any) incurred per unit increase in partner industrial production, than does non-discriminatory reciprocal tariff reduction. On the other hand, preferential tariff reduction imposes an additional cost on the tariff reducing country: the excess of the costs of imports from the partner country over their cost in the world market.

The implications of this analysis are:

(i) both trade creation and trade diversion yield a gain to the customs union partners;

(ii) trade diversion is preferable to trade creation for the preference granting country since a sacrifice of domestic industrial production is not required;

(iii) both trade creation and trade diversion may lead to increased efficiency due to economies of scale.

Johnson's contribution has not achieved the popularity it deserves because of the alleged nature of his assumptions. However, a careful consideration of these assumptions indicates that they are neither extreme nor unique: they are the kind of assumptions that are adopted in any analysis dealing with differences between social and private costs and benefits. It can, of course, be claimed that an "...economic rationale for customs unions on public goods grounds can only be established if for political or some such reasons governments are denied the use of direct production subsidies – and while this may be the case in certain countries at certain periods in their economic evolution, there would appear to be no acceptable reason why this should generally be true. Johnson's analysis demonstrates that customs union and other acts of commercial policy may make economic sense under certain restricted conditions, but in no way does it establish or seek to establish a general argument for these acts" (Krauss 1972, p. 428).

While this is a legitimate criticism, it is of no relevance to the world we live in: subsidies are superior to tariffs, yet all countries prefer the use of tariffs to subsidies. It is a criticism related to a first-best view of the world. Therefore, it seems unfair to criticise an analysis on grounds which do not portray what actually exists; it is what prevails in practice that matters. That is what Johnson's approach is all about and that is what the theory of second-best tries to tackle. In short, the lack of belief in this approach is tantamount to a lack of belief in the validity of the distinction between social and private costs and benefits.

4. Dynamic effects.

The so-called dynamic effects (Balassa 1962) relate to the numerous means by which economic integration may influence the rate of growth of GNP of the participating nations. These ways include the following:

(a) scale economies made possible by the increased size of the market for both firms and industries operating below optimum capacity before integration occurs;

(b) economies external to the firm and industry which may have a downward influence on both specific and general cost structures;

(c) the polarisation effect, by which is meant the cumulative decline either in relative or absolute terms of the economic situation of a particular participating nation or of a specific region within it due either to the benefits of trade creation becoming concentrated in one region or to the fact that an area may develop a tendency to attract factors of production;

(d) the influence on the location and volume of real investment; and

(e) the effect on economic efficiency and the smoothness with which trade transactions are carried out due to enhanced competition and changes in uncertainty.

Hence these dynamic effects include various and completely different phenomena. Apart from economies of scale, the possible gains are extremely long term in nature and cannot be tackled in orthodox economic terms: for example, intensified competition leading to the adoption of best business practices and to an American-type of attitude, etc. (Scitovsky 1958) seems like a naive socio-psychological abstraction that has no solid foundation with regard to both the aspirations of those countries contemplating economic integration and to its actually materialising.

Economies of scale can, however, be analysed in orthodox economic terms. In a highly simplistic model, like that depicted in figure 11.3 where scale economies are internal to the industry, their effects can easily be demonstrated. $D_{H,P}$ is the identical demand curve for this commodity in both H and P and D_{H+P} is their joint demand curve; S_W is the world supply curve; AC_P and AC_H are the average cost curves for this commodity in P and H respectively. Note that the diagram is drawn in such a manner that W has constant average costs and that it is the most efficient supplier of this commodity. Hence free trade is the best policy resulting in price OA with consumption which is satisfied entirely by imports of Oq_4 in each of H and P giving a total of Oq_6.

If H and P impose tariffs, the only justification for this is that uncorrected distortions exist between the privately and socially valued costs in these countries – see Jones (1979) and El-Agraa and Jones (1981). The best tariff rates to impose are Corden's (1972) made-to-measure tariffs which can be defined as those which encourage domestic production to a level that just satisfies domestic consumption without giving rise to monopoly profits. These tariffs are equal to AD and AC for H and P respectively, resulting in Oq_1 and Oq_2 production in H and P respectively.

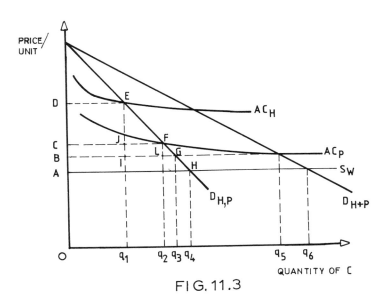

FIG. 11.3

When H and P enter into a customs union, P, being the cheaper producer, will produce the entire union output - Oq_5 at a price OB. Note that this requires a common external tariff rate of AB/OA, i.e. a lower tariff than initially in the more efficient partner. This gives rise to consumption in each of H and P of Oq_3 with gains of BDEG and BCFG for H and P respectively. Parts of these gains, BDEI for H and BCFL for P, are 'cost-reduction' effects, i.e. the initial cost of this amount has been reduced due to economies of scale. There also results a production gain for P and a production loss in H due to abandoning production altogether.

Whether customs union formation can be justified in terms of the existence of economies of scale will depend on whether the net effect is a gain or a loss (in this example P gains and H loses), as the loss from abandoning production in H must outweigh the consumption gain in order for the tariff to have been imposed in the first place. If the overall result is net gain, then the <u>distribution</u> of these gains becomes an important consideration. Alternatively, if economies of scale accrue to an integrated industry, then the <u>locational distribution</u> of the production units becomes an essential issue.

5. The terms of trade effects.

So far the analysis has been conducted on the assumption that customs union formation has no effect on the terms of trade, which implies that the countries concerned are too insignific- ant to have any appreciable influence on the international economy. Particularly in the context of the EC and groupings of a similar size, this is a very unrealistic assumption.

The analysis of the effects of customs union formation on the terms of trade is not only extremely complicated but is also unsatisfactory since a convincing model incorporating tariffs by all three countries is still awaited - see Mundell (1964), Arndt (1968) and Wonnacott and Wonnacott (1981). At this level of generality, however, it suffices to state that nations acting in consort or in unison are more likely to exert an influence than each acting alone. It could also be argued that the bigger the group the stronger its bargaining position vis-a-vis the outside world. Indeed, Petith (1977) found evidence of improved terms of trade for the EC.

It should be stressed, however, that possible gains from improved terms of trade can be achieved only if the outside world does not retaliate. Indeed, the gains found by Petith for the EC could be attributed entirely to this factor. Hence, larger groupings do not necessarily automatically guarantee favourable changes in the terms of trade since such groupings may also encourage joint action by those nations excluded from them.

Theory of Economic Integration

Customs Unions versus Free Trade Areas

The analysis so far has been conducted on the premise that differences between customs unions and free trade areas can be ignored. However, the ability of the member nations of free trade areas to decide their own commercial policies vis-a-vis the outside world raises certain issues. Balassa (1962) pointed out that free trade areas may result in deflection of trade, production and investment. Deflection of trade occurs when imports from W (the cheapest source of supply) come via the member country with the lower tariff rate, assuming that transport and administrative costs do not outweight the tariff differential. Deflection of production and investment occurs in commodities whose production requires a substantial quantity of raw materials imported from W — the tariff differential regarding these materials might distort the true comparative advantage in domestic materials therefore resulting in resource allocations according to overall comparative disadvantage.

If deflection of trade occurs, the free trade area effectively becomes a customs union with a CET equal to the lowest tariff rate, which is obviously beneficial for the world — see Curzon (1974 and 1982). However, most free trade areas seem to adopt 'rules of origin' so that only those commodities which originate in a member state are exempt from tariff imposition. If deflection of production and investment takes place, we have the case of the so-called 'tariff factories' but the necessary conditions for this are extremely limited — see El-Agraa in El-Agraa and Jones (1981, chapter 3).

Economic Unions

The analysis of customs unions needs drastic extension when applied to economic unions. Firstly, the introduction of free factor mobility may enhance efficiency through a more efficient allocation of resources but it may also lead to depressed areas and therefore create, or aggravate, regional problems and imbalances. Secondly, fiscal harmonisation may also improve efficiency by eliminating non-tariff trade distortions and by subjecting factors of production to equal treatment hence encouraging their efficient mobility. Thirdly, the coordination of monetary and fiscal policies implied by monetary integration eases unnecessarily severe imbalances hence promoting the right atmosphere for stability in the economies of member nations.

These 'economic union' elements must be considered <u>simultaneously</u> with trade creation and trade diversion. However, such interactions are too complicated to consider here; the interested reader should consult El-Agraa (1980).

General Equilibrium Analysis

The conclusions of the partial equilibrium analysis can easily

be illustrated in general equilibrium terms. To simplify the
analysis we shall assume that H is a 'small' country while P
and W are 'large' countries, i.e. H faces constant t/t (t_p and
t_w) throughout the analysis. Also, in order to avoid repetition, the analysis proceeds immediately to the Cooper/Massell
approach.

In figure 11.4, HH is the PPF for H. Initially, H is
imposing a prohibitive non-discriminatory tariff which results
in P_1 as both the production and consumption point, given that
t_w is the most favourable t/t, i.e. W is the most efficient
country in the production of Clothing. The formation of the
customs union leads to free trade with the partner (P), hence
production moves to P_2 where t_p is at a tangent to HH, and
consumption to C_3 where CIC_5 is at a tangent to t_p. A unilateral tariff reduction which results in P_2 as the production
point results in consumption at C_4 on CIC_6 (if the tariff
revenue is returned to the consumers as a lump-sum) or at C_3
(if the tariff revenue is retained by the government). Note
that at C_4 trade is with W only.

Given the analysis in chapter 8, it should be apparent
that the situation of unilateral tariff reduction and trade
with W results in exports of AP_2 which are exchanged for imports of AC_4 of which C_3C_4 is the tariff revenue. In terms of
Johnson's distinction between consumption and production gains
(chapter 4) and his method of calculating them (chapter 10),
these effects can be expressed in terms of Food only. Given

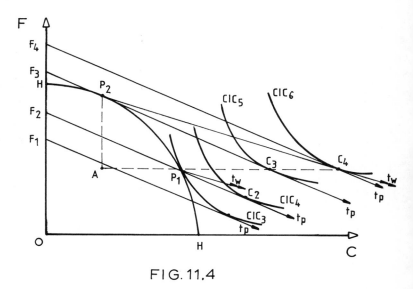

FIG. 11.4

a Hicksian income compensation variation, it should be clear
that: (i) f_1f_2 is the positive consumption effect; (ii) f_2f_3
is the production effect (positive due to curtailing production
of the protected commodity); and (iii) f_3f_4 is the tariff
revenue effect. Hence the difference between customs union
formation and a unilateral tariff reduction (with the tariff
revenue returned to the consumer) is the loss of tariff
revenue f_3f_4 (C_4 compared with C_3). In other words, the consumption gain f_1f_2 is positive and applies in both cases but
in the Cooper/Massell analysis the production effect comprises
two parts: (i) a <u>pure</u> trade creation effect equal to f_2f_4;
and (ii) a <u>pure</u> trade diversion effect equal to f_3f_4. Hence
f_2f_3 is the difference between these two effects and is,
therefore, rightly termed the <u>net</u> trade creation effect.

Of course, the above analysis falls short of a general
equilibrium one since the model does not endogenously determine the t/t - see chapter 5. However, as suggested above,
such an analysis would require the use of offer curves for all
three countries both with and without tariffs. Unfortunately
such an analysis is still awaited - the attempt by Vanek (1965)
to derive an 'excess offer curve' for the potential union
partners leads to no more than a specification of various
possibilities; and the contention of Wonnacott and Wonnacott
(1981) to have provided an analysis incorporating a tariff by
W is unsatisfactory since they assume that W's offer curve
is perfectly elastic. Therefore, at this stage of development
it is not worth devoting space to this aspect of the subject,
even though the topic is an extremely important one. However,
the conclusions of the above section still remain valid since
no rigorous analysis is ever likely to alter them.

Macroeconomics of Integration

We have seen that trade creation and trade diversion are the
two concepts most widely used in international economic integration. We have also seen that their economic implications
for resource reallocation are usually tackled in terms of
particular commodities under conditions of global full employment. However, the economic consequences for the outside
world and their repercussions on the integrated area are
usually left to intuition. Moreover, their implications for
employment are usually ruled out by assumption.

In an effort to rectify these serious shortcomings, I
have used a macroeconomic model (see chapters 6-8 of El-Agraa
and Jones 1981) with the purpose of investigating these aspects. The initial model has been improved and a sophisticated
version has just been published (Jones 1982). However, the
sophistication has left the conclusions of the crude model
still intact. The analysis indicates that the advantages of
using a macro model are that it clearly demonstrates the once-
and-for-all nature of trade creation and trade diversion. It

shows the insignificance of their overall impact given realistic values of the relevant coefficients: marginal propensities to import; marginal propensities to consume; tariff rates, etc. In addition, the model demonstrates that trade creation is beneficial for the partner gaining the new output and exports but is detrimental to the other partner and the outside world; also that trade diversion is beneficial for the partner now exporting the commodity but is detrimental for the other partner and the outside world. The author feels that yet further sophistication of the model will corroborate these conclusions.

Economic Integration among Communist Countries

The only example up to now of economic integration among communist countries is the CMEA - Council for Mutual Economic Assistance or COMECON as it is generally known in the West. However, here the economic system perpetuates a fundamental lack of interest of domestic producers in becoming integrated with both consumers and producers in other member countries. The integration policies of member nations must focus on the mechanism of state-to-state relations rather than on domestic economic policies which would make CMEA integration more attractive to producers and consumers alike. That is, integration must be planned by the state at the highest possible level and imposed on ministries, trusts and enterprises. It should also be stated that the CMEA operates different pricing mechanisms for intra- and extra-area trade. Moreover, the attitude of the USSR is extremely important since the policies of the East European members of the CMEA are somewhat constrained by the policies adopted by the organisation's most powerful member, for economic as well as political reasons. CMEA integration, therefore, has to be approached within an entirely different framework; this is, therefore, not the appropriate place for discussing it - the interested reader should consult Marer and Montias (1982).

Economic Integration among Developing Countries

It has been claimed that the body of economic integration theory as so far developed has no relevance for the Third World due to the fact that the theory suggested that there would be more scope for trade creation if the countries concerned were initially very competitive in production but potentially very complementary and that a customs union would be more likely to be trade creating if the partners conducted most of their foreign trade amongst themselves - see Lipsey (1960) and Meade (1955). These conditions are unlikely to be satisfied in the majority of the developing nations. Moreover, most of the effects of integration are initially bound to be trade diverting, particularly since most of the Third World seeks to industrialise.

On the other hand, it was also realised that an important obstacle to the development of industry in these countries is the inadequate size of their individual markets – see Brown (1961), Hazlewood (1967 and 1975) and Robson (1980). It is therefore necessary to increase the market size so as to encourage optimum plant installations – hence the need for economic integration. This would, however, result in industries clustering together in the relatively more advanced of these nations – those that have already commenced the process of industrialisation.

I have demonstrated elsewhere (El-Agraa 1979a and chapter 6 of El-Agraa and Jones 1981) that there is essentially no theoretical difference between economic integration in the Advanced World and the Third World but that there is a major difference in terms of the type of economic integration that is politically feasible: the need for an equitable distribution of the gains from industrialisation and the location of industries is an important issue (see above). This suggests that any type of economic integration being contemplated must incorporate as an essential element a common fiscal authority and some coordination of economic policies. But then one could equally well argue that some degree of these elements is necessary in any type of integration – see the Raisman Committee recommendations for the EAC (1961), El-Agraa (1982), Hazlewood in El-Agraa (1982).

Conclusions

The conclusions reached here are consistent with my (1979a) conclusions and with those of Jones in El-Agraa and Jones (1981); the contributions by Dixit (1975), Berglas (1979), Collier (1979), Riezman (1979), Whalley (1979), McMillan and McCann (1981) and Wonnacott and Wonnacott (1981) do not affect these conclusions sufficiently to merit separate consideration. They are :

Firstly, that the rationale for regional economic integration rests upon the existence of constraints on the use of first-best policy instruments. Economic analysis has had little to say about the nature of these constraints, and presumably the evaluation of any regional scheme of economic integration should incorporate a consideration of the validity of the view that such constraints do exist to justify the pursuit of second- rather than first-best solutions.

Secondly, that even when the existence of constraints on superior policy instruments is acknowledged, it is misleading to identify the results of regional economic integration by comparing an arbitrarily chosen common policy with an arbitrarily chosen national policy. Of course ignorance and inertia provide sufficient reasons why existing policies may be non-optimal but it is clearly wrong to attribute gains which would have been achieved by appropriate unilateral action to a policy of regional integration. Equally, although it is appropriate to use the optimal common policy as a point of reference, it must be recognised that this may overstate the gains to be achieved if, as seems highly likely, constraints and inefficiencies in the political processes by which policies are agreed prove to be greater among a group of countries than within any individual country.

Although the first two conclusions raise doubts about the case for regional economic integration, a strong general case for economic integration does exsit, in principle at least. In unions where economies of scale may be in part external to national industries, the rationale for unions rests essentially upon the recognition of the externalities and market imperfections which extend beyond the boundaries of national states. In such circumstances, unilateral national action will not be optimal whilst integrated action offers the scope for potential gain.

As with the solution to most problems of externalities and market imperfections, however, customs union theory frequently illustrates the proposition that a major stumbling block to obtaining the gains from joint optimal action lies in agreeing an acceptable distribution of such gains. Thus the fourth conclusion is that the achievement of the potential gains from economic integration will be limited to countries able and willing to co-operate to distribute these gains so that all partners may benefit compared to the results achieved by independent action. It is easy to argue from this that regional economic integration may be more readily achieved than global solutions but, as the debate about monetary integration in the EC illustrates, the chances of obtaining potential mutual gains may well founder in the presence of disparate views about the distribution of such gains and weak arrangements for redistribution.

Chapter Twelve

ECONOMIC GROWTH AND INTERNATIONAL TRADE

Introduction

The topic of economic growth and international trade tries to
tackle such interesting questions as: what causes economic
growth? what is the effect of economic growth on the pattern
and composition of international trade? does a country share
the benefits of its economic growth with other countries, i.e.
does economic growth affect the terms of trade (t/t)? if
economic growth does affect the t/t adversely, is it possible
for the t/t effect to outweigh the benefits of economic growth,
i.e. is it possible for a country to end up worse off as a
result of economic growth? does international trade affect
economic growth? and all the familiar questions regarding the
effects of economic growth on factor payments, income distribution, etc. That is why the topic forms a substantial part
of the theory of international trade and a proper analysis of
the subject would require a whole book. However, at this
level of exposition one can justifiably be highly selective
with regard to the issues requiring specific discussion; the
purpose of this chapter is, therefore, to do precisely that in
a very brief and concise manner.

The Causes of Economic Growth

Basically, there are two sources of economic growth. Firstly,
since it is assumed that each country is endowed with given
factors of production and technical knowledge, it is obvious
that accumulation of factors and improvements in technology
are a source of economic growth. Secondly, a sudden increase
in the foreign demand for a country's exports, particularly in
the presence of unemployment, is obviously a source of growth —
this is usually referred to as 'export-led' growth.

     With regard to growth in factor endowments, it should be
apparent that populations grow over time and, given certain
institutional arrangements in each country, this may affect
the size of the country's labour force. Fortunately, some

limited aspects of the repercussions of such growth were
tackled in chapter 7 (the Rybczynski theorem), hence one need
not discuss them here. However, it should be stressed that
population growth creates certain problems since a distinction
must be made between this and growth in per capita income: it
should be obvious that a growth in population which results in
the lowering of per capita incomes will necessarily generate
different effects when compared with growth which effectively
increases the size of the country's labour force.

Capital accumulation is of course due to positive investment over time. The increase in the size of a country's capital
stock, given the size of the country's labour force, means
that each worker is aided with more capital over time. Hence
labour productivity rises and with it per capita income. Needless to add that the Rybczynski theorem also applies here.

Finally, technical progress as a result of R & D will of
course affect the country's production possibility frontier
(PPF) by shifting it outwards. The precise nature of the
shift will be determined by whether technical progress applies
to one or both industries, and if it applies to both, whether
or not its overall effect is neutral. This is due to the fact
that technical progress could be L-saving, K-saving or both.
To simplify later discussion, all one needs to know is the
exact nature of the shift in the PPF; this will be dealt with
as and when it arises.

Growth and the t/t

The Rybczynski theorem considered the effects of factor accumulation on the total output of the two commodities in conditions
of constant commodity and factor prices, i.e. given constant
t/t. This indicates that the analysis is not a general equilibrium one since it fails to take into consideration this
crucial factor. The interesting question is: what happens to
the t/t as a result of economic growth?

At this juncture it should be pointed out that serious
analysis of the effects of economic growth on the t/t was
undertaken only after World War II (Batra 1973, p.129) with
the impetus provided mainly by a celebrated but highly crit-
icised article by Hicks (1953) - see Corden (1956 and 1965).
Now, to highlight the issues involved and to simplify the
analysis without any loss of generality, it is usually assumed
that only the home country (H) experiences growth while the
outside world (W) remains stationary. This means that W's
offer curve (OO*) remains constant while H's offer curve (OO)
is displaced as a consequence of economic growth. It should
be clear from the analysis in chapter 5 that the exact dis-
placement of OO will depend on the effect of economic growth
on both supply and demand conditions.

To illustrate the point consider figure 12.1 where HH is
H's pre-growth PPF and H'H' is the post-growth PPF. HH and

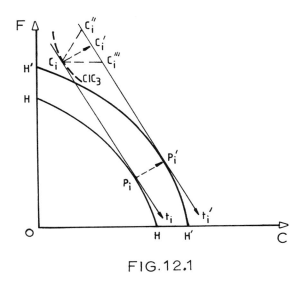

FIG.12.1

H'H' are drawn such that economic growth expands the output of
both Food (F) and Clothing (C) in equal proportions. Before
economic growth is experienced, H is producing at P_i and consuming at C_i, given the t/t depicted by t_i. To analyse what
happens to the t/t eventually, one needs to consider changes
in the supply of F and C as well as changes in the demand for
them on the assumption that t_i remains constant after economic
growth. Hence t_i' is parallel to t_i and the post-growth production point is P_i' indicating an increase in the output of
both F and C. The important question is: what happens to the
consumption point?

If the new consumption point is that depicted by C_i' so
that the distances P_iC_i and $P_i'C_i'$ are equal, i.e. P_iP_i' is
parallel to C_iC_i', the effect of economic growth on H's exports
and imports is nil, hence OO remains constant and so do the
t/t. This result can come about only if the marginal propensity to consume importables in H is equal to the rate of
change in the output of the importable commodity as a proportion of the rate of change in income due to economic growth.
It follows that if the new consumption point is to the north-
west along t_i' (e.g. C_i''), the change in demand for F exceeds
the <u>appropriate</u> rate of change in its output and the t/t will
move against H. The t/t would. of course, improve for H if
the consumption point were C_i'''.

Immiserizing Growth

In the previous section a general case of economic growth,
without specifying the source of growth, was considered, i.e.
growth in both F and C. Now, assume that growth takes place
only in the exportable commodity (C). The increased output of
C will have to be disposed of and one incentive will be to reduce its unit price (P_C). Given the unit price of F (P_F), it
follows that the t/t (i.e. P_C/P_F) must fall. Hence the t/t
must deteriorate if the country experiences growth only in its
exportable commodity and if W remains static in the meantime.
What is of particular interest is whether or not the worsening
of the t/t (i.e. the lowering of real income) for the growth
experiencing country leaves that country worse off as a result.
    Before answering this question it is very important to
point out that the issue raised here is not the one of economic
growth leading to pollution, increased congestion and the rise
of crime in urban areas, i.e. is not whether economic growth is
worth seeking. What is at issue is whether economic growth in
a commodity which is a 'good', not a 'bad' or 'neuter', can
actually lead to a lowering in per capita income, i.e. in real
income, in the country experiencing growth. This point needs
emphasising since it is easy to fall into the trap of confusing
the two.
    This main issue can be meaningfully discussed with refer-
ence to figure 12.2. In the diagram HH is H's pre-growth PPF

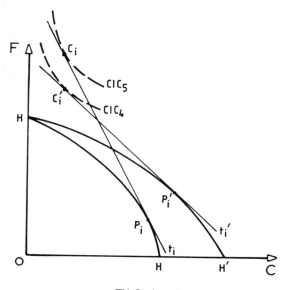

FIG.12.2

with H producing at P_i and consuming at C_i given the t/t depicted by t_i. The difference between consumption and production is satisfied via international trade such that H exports
C and imports F as determined by the length of the distance
C_iP_i along t_i.

When growth takes place in the C industry, it is assumed
that this will displace the PPF to HH' and result in the deterioration in the t/t as indicated by t_i'. Production is
now at P_i' and consumption at C_i'. As the diagram is drawn, it
can be seen that H's new level of community satisfaction (CIC4)
is lower than the initial level (CIC5). Hence, H has become
worse off as a result of economic growth: H's real income has
been lowered. This interesting result is referred to as
'immiserizing growth' and is usually attributed to Bhagwati
(1958) due to his precise formulation of it, but it was recognised earlier by Johnson (1953 and 1955).

It should be noted that this is an extreme outcome since
the post-growth t/t need not worsen so much as to result in a
deterioration in H's economic welfare; the reader should by now
be able to depict such positions on figure 12.2. It should
also be apparent that economic growth need not occur only in C;
the whole of HH could move outwards but biased in favour of C.

Since 'immiserizing growth' is a significant result, let
us restate its necessary preconditions. Firstly, economic
growth essentially increases the capacity and output of the
growing country's exportable sector. Secondly, the foreign
price elasticities of demand for the growing country's exportable commodity must be extremely low. These two conditions,
taken together, ensure that the country's export supply is
increased at the global level and that the t/t must deteriorate
drastically in order that world markets should be cleared.
However, one needs to ask about the practical relevance of
'immiserizing growth'.

In the case of a 'small' country, the effects of growth on
the t/t can be ignored altogether by assumption, hence economic
growth must necessarily benefit such a country. In the case
of a 'large' country, there is the possibility of economic
growth in the importable sector, and it should be obvious from
the above discussion that such growth will lead to an improvement in the t/t hence resulting in a reinforcement of the
benefits of economic growth. In practical terms, it is therefore necessary to find out which commodities have very low
price elasticities in their foreign demand. It should be
apparent that such commodities are necessarily basically agricultural products or certain intermediate products and raw
materials, e.g. coffee, cotton, etc. These are essentially
the exports of developing countries, most of which are 'small'
countries. Hence, the practical feasibility of 'immiserizing
growth' is confined to 'large' developing countries.

Finally, it should be pointed out that some trade theorists
have interpreted the case of 'immiserizing growth' in policy

terms to mean that developing countries should channel their investment towards import-competing industries and away from the export sector. However, the fallacious nature of such an across-the-board policy recommendation should by now be apparent to the reader: 'immiserizing growth' can take place only if the developing country under consideration can influence the t/t.

Growth under Protection

So far the analysis of economic growth has been conducted under conditions of free trade both before and after growth. The discussion of trade impediments in chapters 8–10 clearly demonstrated that certain developing countries may be justified in protecting certain industries, albeit under very restrictive assumptions. This raises the issue regarding the effect of economic growth on a developing country which is adopting a trade impediment to protect its import-competing industry. This is a topic which warrants consideration particularly since in the past few years there has been a general revival of interest in protectionism – see Godley and Cripps (1976), Godley and May (1977), Godley (1981), my criticism of their work (El-Agraa 1982a and 1982b) and Page (1981) for recent developments in protectionism.

Johnson (1967) was the first trade theorist to consider this case. His analysis can be clearly explained with reference to figure 12.3 where HH depicts H's pre-growth PPF. H is assumed to face constant t/t such as t_f^2, hence H is a 'small' country. H imposes a tariff on F thus raising the domestic price ratio to t_d^1. Given t_d^1 and t_f^2, H's production and consumption points are, respectively, P_1 and C_2. H is, therefore, an importer of F and an exporter of C.

The protection afforded to F is designed to enable the industry to grow and this displaces the PPF to H'H' in a manner biased towards F production. After economic growth has occurred, H is assumed to continue to protect its importable commodity and to trade at the given t/t. Hence, the post-growth production and consumption points are, respectively, P_2 and C_1 – note that t_d^2 and t_f^1 are, respectively, parallel to t_d^1 and t_f^2. Since C_1 depicts a lower level of economic welfare than C_2 (CIC_4 compared with CIC_5), H has become worse off as a result of economic growth in the face of protectionism and constant t/t.

Note that if protection is removed after economic growth has been achieved, the new production and consumption points will be determined by the tangency of a line parallel to t_i to both H'H' and a CIC; it should be obvious that such points will result in H reaching a higher CIC than CIC_5. Hence the policy implications of the analysis should be too obvious to warrant any consideration particularly if one notes the affinity of this analysis to that of the 'infant industry' argument.

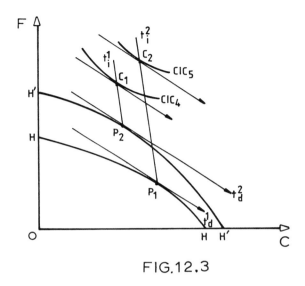

FIG.12.3

Trade and Growth

One final issue that should be of interest is that concerning the effect of international trade on economic growth. As indicated earlier, a sudden shift in foreign demand favouring a country's exportable commodity could lead to economic growth in that country, hence the concept of 'export-led' growth recently revived by Thirlwall and Dixon (1979) and Thirlwall (1979, 1980 and 1982). Of course, the shift in foreign demand could be engineered by H itself adopting commercial practices that produce the desired result.

This analysis need not be pursued here since its general equilibrium implications are similar to those discussed above under general considerations.

Conclusion

As indicated in the introduction, the subject of economic growth and international trade forms a substantial part of the theory of international trade. Given the nature of this book, therefore, one has to be very selective with regard to the issues raised. However, the interested reader should consult the Bibliography and the references given in the books and articles listed there. The advanced reader should consult such texts as Chacholiades (1978).

153

Chapter Thirteen

MARKET IMPERFECTIONS AND FACTOR MOBILITY

Introduction

The analysis in the major part of this book has been conducted
on the basis of three broad assumptions. Firstly, it is
assumed throughout that factors of production, though perfectly
mobile <u>within</u> countries, are perfectly immobile <u>between</u> them.
Secondly, except in the cases of commodity and factor market
distortions discussed in chapters 10 and 11 and some of the
discussion in chapter 6, that both factor and commodity markets
operate under conditions of perfect (atomistic) competition.
Thirdly, that there are no transportation costs. The purpose
of this chapter is to consider some of the interesting topics
that arise as a result of relaxing these assumptions.

It should be pointed out that more recently there have
emerged a number of valuable contributions incorporating
the relaxation of the assumptions of atomistic competition in
factor and commodity markets and that the question of factor
mobility at the international level has been present, albeit
in a disguised manner - see below - for a long time (see the
protracted discussion between Keynes and Ohlin in the <u>Economic
Journal</u> in the 1920s and 1930s). One, therefore, has to be
very selective with regard to which topics to consider given
this level of exposition.

With regard to transportation costs, it should be obvious
that in some instances they will eliminate international trade
altogether or simply reduce its volume by increasing the effective unit cost in the importing country. There is therefore no
need to spend valuable space discussing the obvious particularly
since some elements of transportation costs were considered in
chapters 6 and 11.

Market Imperfections

The relaxation of the assumption of perfect competition in production calls for an examination of the behaviour, at the
national level, of firms operating under conditions of

monopolistic and oligopolistic market structures, and, at the international level, of multinational firms and cartels (e.g. OPEC). First, consider the question of the gains from trade when a country (H) has a domestic monopoly in its Food (F) industry.

From a knowledge of general economics, the reader should be familiar with the notion that a profit maximising monopolist equates marginal cost (MC) and marginal revenue (MR) in order to determine the output level. Hence, in comparison with perfect competition, a monopolist produces a lower level of output and charges a higher price per unit in selling it. Now, consider the implications of this for international trade.

In figure 13.1, the autarkic equilibrium position, in the presence of perfect competition in both the F and Clothing (C) industries, is depicted as in chapter 4, i.e. both production and consumption are at point z where H's production possibility frontier (PPF), that depicted by HH, is at a tangent to a community indifference curve (CIC_3) with the slope of the tangent (not drawn) indicating the domestic price ratio, t_d. The existence of monopoly in F means that the autarkic output of F will be less than that given by point z: it could be z_1 or z_2. Note that at z_1 (z_2), t_d will be given by the slope of CIC_2 (CIC_1) at that point (z_1 or z_2). Since either slope is steeper than that at z, this satisfies the condition that a unit of F is more expensive in the presence of monopoly as compared with perfect competition.

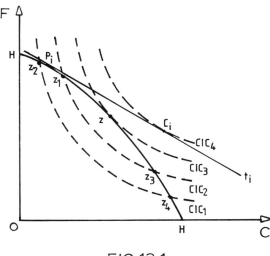

FIG. 13.1

Now, suppose that H is opened up to free international trade at given terms of trade (t/t), those indicated by t_i, i.e. F is cheaper and C is more expensive at the international level when compared with the domestic level. The assumption of given t/t means that the domestic monopolist can now sell only at the going market price, hence the domestic monopolist has become a perfect competitor as a result of international trade. Consequently, the monopolist opts for the output of F given by point P_i (where t_i is at a tangent to HH). The implication of this is that the monopolist either contracts output (if production was initially at z_1) due to the comparatively high domestic costs, or expands output (if production was initially at point z_2) if the domestic costs are not comparatively too high since it would no longer be possible for the monopolist to raise the price by curtailing output.

The interesting point to note is that although H achieves the familiar free trade equilibrium position with output at P_i and consumption at C_i, the gains from trade exceed the usual gains (those in the absence of a domestic monopolist): in the case of monopoly in F, free trade takes H from z to P_i and C_i (from CIC_3 to CIC_4), but with monopoly, free trade takes H from either z_2 or z_1 to P_i and C_i (from either CIC_1 or CIC_2 to CIC_4).

It is appropriate to ask: what if the monopolist is in the C industry (the potential export)? A second glance at figure 13.1 clearly indicates that in autarky output could for instance be at either z_3 or z_4 with the respective t_ds determined as previously. The only difference here is that subjecting the monopolist to free trade at given t/t (t_i) will induce an expansion in the output of C since the monopolist must sell at the same price at both the domestic and international levels. Hence, the previous conclusions are still valid, with the only difference being that t_d (as determined at z_3 or z_4) could be steeper or flatter than t_i due to the fact that international trade may lead to either a fall or a rise in the domestic price of C: if H's comparative advantage is vast then, given that the monopolist has low costs, profit maximisation may necessitate a raising of the domestic price; alternatively, fierce competition at the international level may force a lowering of the domestic price (see Caves and Jones 1981, chapter 9).

Other Imperfections

The previous section was concerned with the cases of monopoly in either industry and in only one country; in the real world there exist oligopolies both at the national and international levels. It is therefore appropriate to ask: how does the existence of oligopolies affect international trade? From a knowledge of general economics the reader should be aware that the outcome in such situations cannot be determined without the incorporation of some constraints on the behaviour of the oligopolists. Once one does that, no general theory can be constructed: the outcome is a series of possibilities depending on the specific constraints incorporated. It should therefore be understandable that it is not advisable to indulge in such analysis at this level of exposition. One should point out, however, that international oligopoly has led to 'cartelisation' (e.g. market sharing), particularly between the two World Wars, and to 'dumping', which is being vigorously fought in GATT, where an oligopolist charges a lower price at the international than at the domestic level – see Wares (1977).

Finally, there is the case of product differentiation but this need not be discussed here since its implications are similar to those discussed in chapter 6.

Factor Mobility

In the discussion of the factor price equalisation theorem in chapter 7 it was pointed out that free trade will never result in complete factor price equalisation. The implication of this is that the prevalence of international differences in factor payments should provide an incentive for factors of production to become mobile internationally, a possibility which was ruled out by the assumptions of the basic HOS model. Suppose factors of production do respond to this incentive, what would be the implications of such mobility?

If factors move to the region (country) where they can fetch the highest possible price (more precisely, the highest reward), this will enhance world efficiency as measured by output per head of the world population, i.e. Pareto-optimality conditions will be satisfied at the international level in exactly the same way as they would be nationally. However, the incentive for mobility may be provided by only a few regions with the consequence that some areas may end up being completely depressed. Hence, one has to weigh the social costs in terms of depressed countries against the benefits of enhanced global efficiency in order to reach a conclusion regarding the desir-ability of international factor mobility. Of course, there will always exist the theoretical possibility that if labour (L) emigrates from one country due to its low L rewards, cap-ital (K) may flow into that country to take advantage of the lower L costs there, hence the region need not end up depressed altogether. However, that remains only a theoretical possibil-ity since practical instances are very few indeed. Finally, actual L mobility is a very insignificant percentage of the total L force.

K and technology (T) are of course more mobile at the international level when compared with L. Also, in a world of multinational firms, management and enterprise are relatively more mobile internationally than L. Theoretically speaking, the mobility of K, T and management at the global level should promote the spread of the best possible business practices, hence leading to enhanced world efficiency. However, multi-national firms are sometimes shown to behave in a manner similar to 'cartels' and when one takes into consideration the fact that in the modern world management tends to be divorced from ownership, it becomes increasingly difficult to sustain this conclusion. This is therefore an area where a great deal of research is warranted.

One issue which deserves specific mention is the claim that L mobility depresses the standard of living of the original (resident) population. Assume that: (i) all the existing residents own the same endowment of K; (ii) only one commodity (C) is being produced; (iii) the immigrant L brings with it less K than owned by the resident population; and (iv) there is no international trade. Now consider figure 13.2 where AA' depicts the price of K in terms of L (or vice versa) for the resident community and the lengths of OA and OA' depict their factor endowment.

When immigration occurs, given assumption (iii), the factor endowment changes to BB' such that BB' is flatter than AA' ($AB/OA < A'B'/OA'$). Initially, total output is given by point z_1 on isoquant C_1 and the level of output after immigration is that depicted by point z_3 on isoquant C_3. Hence, immigration has resulted in a higher level of production.

In order to find out what has happened to the resident population one needs to know what has happened to their output

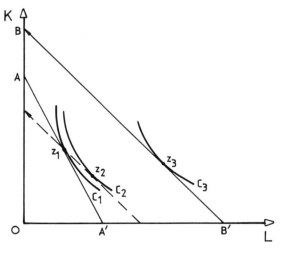

FIG. 13.2

(hence their standard of living) after the immigrants have descended on them. This level of output can be determined by drawing a line parallel to BB' passing through point z. In other words, one needs to introduce a Slutsky income compensation variation. The outcome is that the output of the resident population is that depicted by point z_2 on isoquant C_2. Hence, the standard of living of the resident population has improved in real terms as a consequence of immigration.

It should be apparent from figure 13.2 that as long as immigration leads to a change in the factor price ratio, i.e. the post-immigration endowment line is not parallel to AA', the resident population will gain from immigration. Needless to add that if the factor price ratio is not altered, the resident population maintains its original standard of living. Moreover, as long as there is automatic full employment of L, the resident population can never become worse off, even if the immigrants bring no K at all. Of course, this conclusion cannot be sustained in the case where immigration simply adds to the 'dole queue'.

The Transfer Problem

After the Franco-Prussian war of 1870-71, France was made to provide reparation payments. Germany was asked to do the same after World War I. The USA sent aid (donated a gift) to W. Europe after World War II - the Marshall Plan. W. German capital equipment was stripped after World War II and was relocated in Eastern Europe and the USSR. Canada can borrow in the New York capital market to facilitate a greater accumulation of K equipment there possibly at the expense of the USA. The surpluses of oil-exporting countries are subjected to a 'recycling' process in W. Europe. K, as a factor of production, is transferred from one country to another: what do all these instances have in common?

The answer is simple: they concern the transfer of resources between countries. They also raise the interesting question regarding the effect of such transfers on the t/t. For instance, if the USA made a unilateral resource transfer to W. Europe, would the t/t shift against the USA as a result? If the answer is affirmative, then, in addition to the 'primary burden' of the transfer, there would be a 'secondary burden' for the USA: real income falls not only because of the donation but also because the deterioration in US export prices relative to her import prices depresses the real worth of the remaining national income. Alternatively, could the transfer improve the t/t for the USA? In other words, could it result in a 'secondary blessing'? An affirmative answer here will raise the interesting question regarding whether the 'secondary blessing' exceeds the 'primary burden', i.e. the transfer becomes impossible to effect.

This is a fascinating topic and it is being raised in

this chapter simply because the following analysis applies equally to international K mobility.

In order to simplify the analysis, the basis is assumed to be the HOS model. It is also assumed that: (i) H and W have fixed total supplies of C and F; (ii) initially there are no transfers either way between H and W; and (iii) there is free international trade without transportation costs. The significance of these assumptions is made clear in figure 13.3 where the size of the box is determined by the total joint supplies of C and F and where point z gives their free trade distribution between H and W. z is a point of equilibrium because at that point the two offer curves (OO and O*O*) cross to determine the equilibrium t/t depicted by t_i. Note that at z the CICs for both H and W (not drawn) will be at a tangent to each other with the slope of the tangent being t_i.

Suppose that W donates a gift to H such that the new distribution point becomes z_1. The new offer curves (not drawn) will now intersect at that point giving the new t/t indicated by t_i'. The important question is whether a movement along the contract curve (KK) to the north-east leads to a flatter or steeper t/t, i.e. is t_i' steeper or flatter than t_i. If t_i' is flatter (steeper) than t_i, the t/t would improve (deteriorate) for W indicating a 'secondary burden' ('secondary blessing') for W. Needless to add that if t_i' is parallel to t_i, the transfer will have no secondary effects.

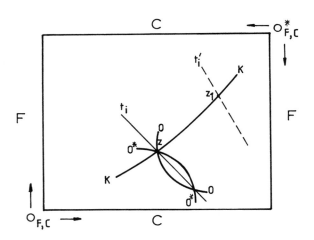

FIG.13.3

A precise answer requires a closer examination of points z and z_1. For this purpose, consider figure 13.4 where points z and z_1 are reproduced but the offer curves have been eliminated. Instead the CICs and the IEPs (income expansion paths or Engel's curves - see chapter 2) have been inserted. Recall that IEPs trace for the relevant set of CICs the points of the same slope. Starting at z_1, as one moves along CIC_8 to the south-east, the slopes along CIC_8 become flatter; the slopes become steeper if one moves along CIC_8 to the north-west. The opposite is true for movements along CIC_2^*. Since KK must be between the two IEPs, it follows that the common slope of CIC_8 and CIC_2^* at z_1 must be steeper than t_i, i.e. t_i' is steeper than t_i. Therefore, the t/t must move against the donating country, i.e. the gift leads to a 'secondary burden'.

Note that the relative slopes of the IEPs are the sole criterion for the impending change in the t/t. Also that only if a movement along a country's IEP causes it to give up the two commodities in <u>exactly the same</u> proportion as the other takes them on will there be no change in the t/t - recall that the necessary condition to produce this result is that the KK must coincide with the diagonal (see chapter 3). It follows that the crucial factors determining the change in the t/t are the marginal physical propensities to consume the two commodities (see Samuelson 1952).

The above analysis is based on the assumption that the initial endowment of F and C is fixed for both H and W. What

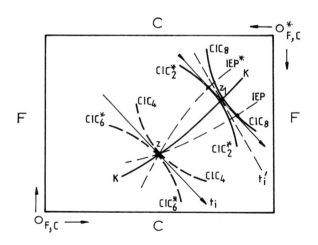

FIG.13.4

if the two countries have normal PPFs? In figure 13.5, HH and WW are the respective initial PPFs for H and W. Let us assume that both supply and demand contract uniformly in the donating country and expand uniformly in the receiving country so that H'H' and W'W' are the post transfer PPFs. Initially, H was producing at point P_1 and consuming at point C_1 with the length of P_1C_1 indicating the level of trade. P_2^* and C_2^* were W's initial production and consumption points with the length $P_2^*C_2^*$ indicating the level of trade. Since this is an international equilibrium situation, it follows that $P_1C_1 = P_2^*C_2^*$, i.e. world trade is in balance.

Now the gift, at constant t/t, results in P_2, P_1^* and C_2, C_1^* as the respective production and consumption points for H and W. Note that P_2C_2 is longer than P_1C_1 (= $P_2^*C_2^*$) while $P_1^*C_1^*$ is shorter. Hence, given constant t/t, the transfer creates an excess supply of F and an excess demand for C. Therefore the relative price of C must rise in order to restore equilibrium conditions, hence the t/t must improve for W, the donor country.

This is of course an extreme case, but hopefully it will help the reader to think about alternative possibilities.

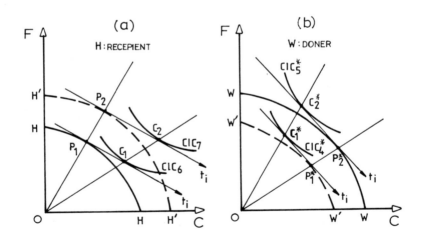

FIG. 13.5

Chapter Fourteen

ECONOMIES OF SCALE

Introduction

The discussion in chapters 3-5 did not take into consideration
the case of economies of scale (increasing returns to scale
or decreasing opportunity costs). The justification is that
the main body of the book deals with cases of increasing
opportunity costs, hence a more thorough analysis of economies
of scale at that stage would have disturbed the reader's
concentration without influencing his ability to follow later
discussion. It should, therefore, be understandable that, in
order to avoid that unfortunate event, this final brief chapter
is devoted to an analysis of that subject.

Economies of Scale and Perfect Competition

From a knowledge of basic economics, particularly of production
functions (PFs) and the theory of the firm, the reader should
be familiar with the notion that economies of scale can be
internal or external to the firm. Recall that internal economies are inconsistent with the assumption of atomistic or perfect competition since their prevalence leads eventually to
one firm becoming so large as to influence the price of its
product. Also, that the concept of external economies is consistent with perfect competition since these occur when all
firms simultaneously experience a lowering in their unit costs
as the level of production is expanded. This could be attributed to pecuniary or technological factors: the former can be
explained by lower factor prices, i.e. lower factor costs, and
the latter by increases in the efficiency with which the firm
operates. It should also be apparent that the pecuniary external economies create no difficulties while technological
external economies do - see Meade (1952), Kemp (1964), Matthews
(1950) and Chacholiades (1978) for a thorough discussion of
these problems.
    Setting these problems aside enables one to consider a
simple case of economies of scale. Assume that a country is in

autarky and that it produces two commodities F and C by utilising a given quantity of K ($\overline{K}$). Also that industry F operates
under conditions of constant opportunity costs and in such a
specific way that the production of 1 unit of F requires 1 unit
of K. Also assume that C is the industry which benefits from
technological external economies. The implications of these
assumptions are depicted in figure 14.1 where: $\overline{OK}$ is the given
endowment of K; the 45° line OZ gives the PF for F; and the
maximum possible output of F, given OZ, is OH, i.e. where the
total endowment of $\overline{K}$ is fully exhausted in the F industry.
Hence, a further implication of these assumptions is that the
quantity of K available to produce C is measured by the vertical
distance between the planned output of F and the maximum
possible output of F (OH). For example, when the planned output of F is equal to OB, then BH of K (equal to $K_1\overline{K}$) is available for C production. Hence, effectively, OH measures not
only the total quantity of K but also its distribution between
F and C. It follows that the axes depicted by DH and OH, with
point H as the origin, determine HH' as the PF for C. Note
that the shape of HH' in relation to these axes reflects the
assumption of technological economies of scale in C. Also
note that HH', when viewed from O as the origin to the axes OF
and OC, is the production possibility frontier (PPF) for the
country.

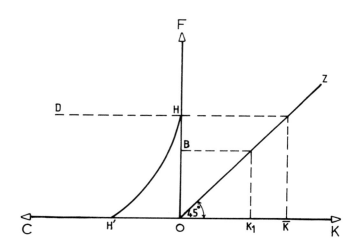

FIG. 14.1

In figure 14.2, the PPF in the left hand quadrant of
figure 14.1 has been reproduced but with the axes in the
normal fashion. Also included in figure 14.2 is the price
expansion path (PEP) of chapters 2 and 3 which necessarily
starts from point H, since country H's budget line must start
there, hence budget line HB is at a tangent to HH at point H.
Therefore, figure 14.2 depicts both the supply and demand conditions for this country.

Recall that efficient production must be on HH' and equilibrium consumption must be on PEP, with the optimum output (E)
being determined by the intersection of HH' and PEP. Note
that at point E the country is not maximising its welfare since
the marginal rate of substitution in consumption (measured by
the slope of line HE – not drawn) exceeds the marginal rate of
transformation in production (measured by the slope of the
tangent – not drawn – to HH' at point E). Hence, appropriate
policy measures have to be undertaken to ensure restoration of
Pareto-optimality conditions – for a rigorous discussion of
these refer to chapter 8 or consult Chacholiades, 1978,
chapters 20 and 21.

The Offer Curve

In order to determine the country's offer curve, it is necessary to specify the country's equilibrium production and consumption points at various price levels (t/t) and to calculate

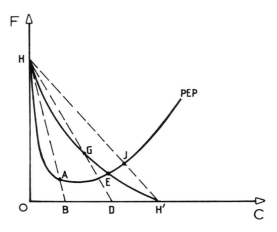

FIG. 14.2

the difference between the two - see chapter 5. The equilibrium consumption points are, of course, all those along PEP
but the determination of the equilibrium production points
needs careful thought.

In order to determine the various equilibrium production
points, it is essential to divide figure 14.2 into 3 areas:
(i) the area within the triangle OHB, i.e. the budget line HB
and steeper budget lines; (ii) the area between HB and the
straight line HH'; and (iii) the area to the right of the
straight line HH, i.e. budget lines flatter than HH'. In
region (i), the price of a unit of C exceeds the ratio of the
average costs of production as determined by the slope of HB
(the tangent to the PPF, HH', at point H). Hence, the production of C is a profitable activity. Since the price of C
rises as one moves in an easterly direction, profitability of
C increases further. Hence, it pays to go all the way to
point H', i.e. to specialise completely in the production of
C. If the price ratio is that depicted by the straight line
HH', production can be at either H or H'. However, it should
be apparent from the discussion of stability conditions in
chapters 3-5 that point H is one of stable while point H' is
one of unstable equilibrium: at point H, the average cost of
production of C is in excess of its price and this applies to
all points except for point H' itself where the price just
covers average costs of production. In this particular sense,
point H is a possible production point since any deviation
from it will generate forces that lead further away from it.
If the relative price ratio is that depicted by line HB itself,
there will be two possible production points: H or H'. However, it should be apparent that at this price ratio, point H
represents an unstable while point H' represents a stable
equilibrium. If the price ratio is in area (iii), country H
will specialise completely in the production of F, i.e. production will be at point H. Finally, if the price ratio lies
in region (ii), line HD for example, there will be three
possible production points (H, G and H') with points H and H'
resulting in a stable and point G in an unstable equilibrium.

Now, given the different possible production and equilibrium consumption points, it should be obvious that the
country's offer curve is determined by the divergencies between
the two. For instance, if the commodity price ratio is flatter
than the straight line HH' in figure 14.2, the country will
specialise in the production of F and import C such that the
offer curve will be a mirror image of PEP to the right of
point J. This is shown more clearly in figure 14.3 where: the
bottom right hand quadrant exactly reproduces figure 14.2;
point H becomes the origin for the remaining three quadrants;
t/t B'B" and H"H''' are respectively equivalent to HB and HH'.
Hence J'K is a mirror image of PEP to the right of J.

If the t/t are those depicted by the straight line HH',
there will be two production points (at H and H') but only one

166

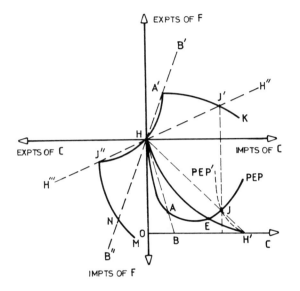

FIG. 14.3

consumption point (at J), hence the country will make two offers. These are depicted by J' and J" in the relevant quadrant, i.e. depending on which commodity is exported and which is imported. For t/t in area (i), country H will specialise in the production of C and consume along PEP', hence the relevant offer curve is NM. If the t/t are equal to the slope of HB, there will be two production points (H and H') and two offers: point N if production is at H' and point A' if production is at point H and consumption at point A. Finally, if the t/t are in area (ii) there will be three possible production points, therefore three offers: if production is at H and consumption is between A and J, the offer

curve will be A'J, i.e. a mirror image of AJ along PEP; if
production is at H' and consumption along J-PEP', the offer
curve is J"N; and if E itself is the point of equilibrium
there are three distinct possibilities - if the line HE is the
t/t, consumption is equal to production, hence H is the point
on the contract curve; if the t/t are between the lines HB
and HE (not drawn), commodity C will be imported while F will
be exported giving HA' as the offer curve; and if the t/t are
between lines HE and HH', C will be exported while F will be
imported and the offer curve will be HJ".

Now, putting all this information together, gives
MNJ"HA'J'K as the offer curve. This is reproduced in figure
14.4 where the original t/t given by B'B" and H"H''' are also
reproduced plus new t/t (xx) at a tangent to the offer curve
at point H, i.e. the autarkic equilibrium price ratio. Now,
the opening of the country to international trade has the
following implications. Firstly, if the international t/t are
flatter than H"H''', the country will specialise in the production of F and import C since the only possible intersection
points are along J'K. Secondly, if the international t/t are
steeper than B'B", the country will specialise in the production of C and import F, since the only possible intersection
points are along NM. Thirdly, in the case where the international t/t are between H"H''' and B'B", there will always be
three intersection points, therefore three trade offers, hence
the country's specialisation in production and its direction of
trade will be indeterminate.

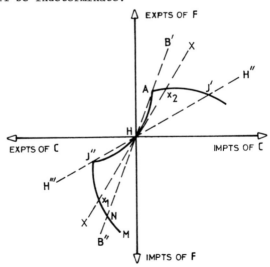

FIG. 14.4

Finally, it should be noted that when the international t/t coincide with xx, there will still be international trade, given the derivation of the offer curve. This, recall, is in sharp contrast to the increasing and constant opportunity cost cases.

Conclusion

In conclusion, the reader should realise that the above analysis can also be applied to the rest of the world (W) in the manner of chapter 5: the rest of the world can be modelled in precisely the same fashion as the above country (H) so that when the two offer curves are drawn (OO and O*O*) they necessarily intersect at three different points – see figure 14.5. Note that points z_1 and z_2 are points of complete specialisation and stable equilibrium while point z_3 is not – this should be obvious from the derivation of the offer curves.

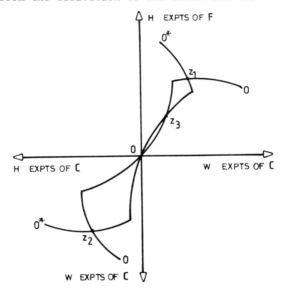

FIG.14.5

A SELECTED BIBLIOGRAPHY

Adams, W. (1968) The Brain Drain (London : Macmillan)
Agarwal, M., Askari, H., and Corson, W. (1975) 'A testing
    of the Ricardian theory of comparative advantage',
    Economia Internazionale, vol. 28
Allen, P. R., and Kenen, P. B. (1980) Asset Markets, Exchange
    Rates and Economic Integration : a Synthesis, Cambridge
    University Press
Allen, W. (ed.) (1965) International Trade Theory : Hume to
    Ohlin (New York : Random House)
Armington, P. S. (1969) 'A theory of demand for products
    distinguished by place of production', IMF Staff Papers,
    March
Arndt, S. W. (1968) 'On discriminatory versus non-preferential
    tariff policies', Economic Journal, vol. 78. Reprinted
    in P. Robson (1972)
Balassa, B. (1961) The Theory of Economic Integration
    (Homewood, Ill. : Irwin)
Balassa, B. (1963) 'An empirical demonstration of classical
    comparative cost theory', Review of Economics and
    Statistics, vol. 45
Balassa, B. (1965) 'Tariff protection in industrial countries :
    an evaluation', Journal of Political Economy, vol. 73
Balassa, B. (1967) 'Trade creation and trade diversion in the
    European Common Market', Economic Journal, vol. 77.
    Reprinted in P. Robson (1972)
Balassa, B. et al. (1974) European Economic Integration
    (Amsterdam : North-Holland)
Baldwin, R. E. (ed.) (1965) Trade, Growth and the Balance of
    Payments (Chicago : Rand McNally)
Baldwin, R. E. (1971a) 'Determinants of the commodity
    structure of US trade', American Economic Review, vol. 61
Baldwin, R. E. (1971b) Non-tariff Distortions of International
    Trade (London : Macmillan)
Barker, P. (1977) 'International cartels in primary commodities',
    in P. Maunder (ed.) Case Studies in International
    Economics (London : Heinemann)

A Selected Bibliography

Batra, R. N., and Pattanaik, P. K. (1971) 'Factor market imperfections and gains from trade', Oxford Economic Papers, vol. 23

Batra, R. N. (1973) Studies in the Pure Theory of International Trade (London : Macmillan)

Batra, R. N., and Avinash, C. S. (1977) 'Unemployment, tariffs and the theory of international trade', Journal of International Economics, vol. 7

Berglas, E. (1979) 'Preferential trading theory : the n commodity case', Journal of Political Economy, vol. 81

Bhagwati, J. N. (1958) 'Immiserizing growth: a geometric note', Review of Economic Studies, vol. 25. Reprinted in Caves and Johnson (1968)

Bhagwati, J. N. (1959) 'Protection, real wages and real incomes', Economic Journal, vol. 69. Reprinted in Bhagwati (1969a)

Bhagwati, J. N. and Ramaswami, V. K. (1963) 'Domestic distortions, tariffs, and the theory of optimum subsidy', Journal of Political Economy, vol. 71

Bhagwati, J. N. (1964) 'The pure theory of international trade: a survey', Economic Journal, vol. 74

Bhagwati, J. N. (1968) The Theory and Practice of Commercial Policy, Princeton University Press

Bhagwati, J. N. (ed.) (1969a) International Trade (Harmondsworth: Penguin)

Bhagwati, J. N. (1969b) 'On the equivalence of tariffs and quotas', in J. N. Bhagwati, Trade, Tariffs and Growth (London : Weidenfeld and Nicholson)

Bhagwati, J. N. (1971a) 'Customs unions and welfare improvement', Economic Journal, vol. 81

Bhagwati, J. N. (1971b) 'The generalised theory of distortions and welfare', in Bhagwati et al. (1971)

Bhagwati, J. N., Jones, R. W., Mundell, R. A., and Vanek, J. (eds) (1971) Trade, Balance of Payments and Growth (Amsterdam : North-Holland)

Bhagwati, J. N., and Srinivasan, T. N. (1973) 'Smuggling and trade policy', Journal of Public Economics, vol 2

Bhagwati, J. N., and Hansen, B. (1973) 'A theoretical analysis of smuggling', Quarterly Journal of Economics, vol. 87

Bhagwati, J. N. (1973) 'The theory of immiserizing growth : further applications', in Connolly and Swoboda (1973)

Bhagwati, J. N. (ed.) (1974) Illegal Transactions in International Trade : Theory and Measurement (Amsterdam : North-Holland)

Bhagwati, J. N., and Srinivasan, T. N. (1980) 'Revenue seeking : a generalisation of the theory of tariffs', Journal of Political Economy, vol. 88

Bharadwaj, R. (1962a) 'Structural basis for India's foreign trade', Series in International and Monetary Economics, no. 6, University of Bombay

171

A Selected Bibliography

Bharadwaj, R. (1962b) 'Factor proportions and the structure of Indo–US trade' Indian Economic Journal, vol. 10

Black, J., and Dunning, J. H. (eds) (1982) International Capital Movements (London : Macmillan)

Brock, W. A., and Magee, S. P. (1978) 'The economics of special interest politics : the case of the tariff', American Economic Review, Papers and Proceedings, vol. 68

Brown, A. J. (1961) 'Economic separatism versus a common market in developing countries', Bulletin of Economic Research, vol. 13

Caves, R. E. (1960) Trade and Economic Structure, Harvard University Press

Caves, R. E., and Johnson, H. G. (eds) (1968) Readings in International Economics (London : Allen and Unwin)

Caves, R. E., and Jones, R. W. (1981) World Trade and Payments : an Introduction (Boston : Little, Brown)

Chacholiades, M. (1978) International Trade Theory and Policy (New York : McGraw-Hill)

Cheh, J. H. (1974) 'United States concessions in the Kennedy Round and short-run labour adjustments costs', Journal of International Economics, vol. 4

Chipman, J. S. (1966) 'A survey of the theory of international trade : part 2, the neo-classical theory', Econometrica, vol. 34

Clement, M. O., Pfister, F. L., and Rothwell, K. J. (1967) Theoretical Issues in International Economics (New York : Houghton Mifflin)

Collier, P. (1979) 'The welfare effects of customs union : an anatomy', Economic Journal, vol. 89

Connolly, M. B., and Swoboda, A. K. (eds) (1973) International Trade Theory (London : Allen and Unwin)

Cooper, C. A., and Massell, B. F. (1965a) 'A new look at customs union theory', Economic Journal, vol. 75

Cooper, C. A., and Massell, B. F. (1965b) 'Towards a general theory of customs unions in developing countries', Journal of Political Economy, vol. 73

Corden, W. M. (1956) 'Economic expansion and international trade : a geometric approach', Oxford Economic Papers, vol. 8

Corden, W. M. (1965) 'Recent developments in the pure theory of international trade', Special Papers in International Economics, no. 7, Princeton University Press

Corden, W. M. (1970) 'The efficiency effects of trade and protection', in I. A. McDougall and R. H. Snape (eds) Studies in International Economics (Amsterdam : North-Holland)

Corden, W. M. (1971a) The Theory of Protection, Oxford University Press

Corden, W. M. (1971b) 'The effect of trade on the rate of growth', in Bhagwati et al. (1971)

Corden, W. M. (1972) 'Economies of scale and customs union

theory', Journal of Political Economy, vol. 80

Corden, W. M. (1974) Trade Policy and Economic Welfare, Oxford University Press

Corden, W. M. (1975) 'The costs and consequences of protection: a survey of empirical work', in P. Kenen (1975)

Curzon, G. and V. (1971) Hidden Barriers to International Trade (London : Macmillan for Trade Policy Research Centre)

Curzon, V. (1974) The Essentials of Economic Integration (London : Macmillan)

Curzon, V. (1982) 'The European Free Trade Association', in A. M. El-Agraa (ed.) International Economic Integration (London : Macmillan)

Denison, E. F. (1967) Why Growth Rates Differ : Post War Experience in Nine Western Countries (Washington : Brookings Institution)

Dixit, A. (1975) 'Welfare effects of tax and price changes', Journal of Public Economics, vol. 4

Dixit, A., and Norman, V. (1980) Theory of International Trade, Cambridge University Press

Downs, A. (1957) 'An economic theory of political action in a democracy', Journal of Political Economy, vol. 65

Dunning, J. H. (1970) Studies in International Investment (London : Allen and Unwin)

Dunning, J. H. (ed.) (1972) International Investment (Harmondsworth : Penguin)

El-Agraa, A. M. (1979a) 'Common markets in developing countries', in J. K. Bowers (ed.) Inflation, Development and Integration : Essays in Honour of A. J. Brown, Leeds University Press

El-Agraa, A. M. (1979b) 'Optimum tariffs, retaliation and international cooperation', Bulletin of Economic Research, vol. 31

El-Agraa, A. M. (1979c) 'On tariff bargaining', Bulletin of Economic Research, vol. 31

El-Agraa, A. M. (ed.) (1980a) The Economics of the European Community (Oxford : Philip Allan)

El-Agraa, A. M. (1981) 'Tariff bargaining : a correction', Bulletin of Economic Research, vol. 33

El-Agraa, A. M., and Jones, A. J. (1981) The Theory of Customs Unions (Oxford : Philip Allan)

El-Agraa, A. M. (1982a) 'Wynne Godley's proposition : a theoretical appraisal', Leeds Discussion Papers, no. 105

El-Agraa, A. M. (1982b) 'Professor Godley's proposition : a macroeconomic appraisal', Leeds Discussion Papers, no. 113

El-Agraa, A. M. (ed.) (1982c) International Economic Integration (London : Macmillan)

El-Agraa, A. M. (ed.) (1983a) Britain within the European Community (London : Macmillan)

El-Agraa, A. M. (1983b) Trade Theory and Policy : some Topical Issues, (London : Macmillan)

Ellis, H. S., and Metzler, L.A. (eds) (1949) Readings in the

Theory of International Trade (Homewood, Ill. : Irwin)

Falvey, R. E. (1978) 'A note on preferential and illegal trade under quantitative restrictions', *Quarterly Journal of Economics*, vol. 92

Findlay, R., and Grubert, H. (1959) 'Factor intensities, technological progress and the terms of trade', *Oxford Economic Papers*, vol. 11. Reprinted in Bhagwati (1969a)

Findlay, R. (1971) *Trade and Specialisation* (Harmondsworth : Penguin)

Findlay, R., and Wallisz, S. (1979) 'Rent-seeking, welfare, and the political economy of restrictions', mimeograph (New York : Columbia University)

Gehrels, F. (1956-57) 'Customs unions from a single country viewpoint', *Review of Economic Studies*, vol. 24

Godley, W., and Cripps, F. (1976) 'A formal analysis of the Cambridge Economic Policy Group model', *Economica*, vol. 43

Godley, W., and May, R. M. (1977) 'The macroeconomic implications of devaluation and import restriction', *Cambridge Economic Policy Review*, no. 3

Godley, W. (1981) 'Protection as the only way to full employment : some notes on the macroeconomic theory of international trade', paper delivered to a conference in Bordeaux, June

Gray, H. P. (1973) 'Senile industry protection : a proposal', *Southern Economic Journal*, vol. 83

Grubel, H. G., and Johnson, H. G. (eds) (1971) *Effective Tariff Protection* (Geneva : GATT)

Grubel, H. G. (1977) *International Economics* (Homewood, Ill. : Irwin)

Grubel, H. G., and Lloyd, P. J. (1975) *Intra-industry Trade* (London : Macmillan)

Haberler, G. (1950) 'Some problems in the pure theory of international trade', *Economic Journal*, vol. 60. Reprinted in Caves and Johnson (1968)

Hagen, E. E. (1958) 'An economic justification of protectionism', *Quarterly Journal of Economics*, vol. 72

Hazlewood, A. (1967) *African Integration and Disintegration*, Oxford University Press

Hazlewood, A. (1975) *Economic Integration : the East African Experience* (London : Heinemann)

Hazlewood, A. (1982) 'The East African Community', in A. M. El-Agraa (ed.) *International Economic Integration* (London : Macmillan)

Heckscher, E. (1919) 'The effects of foreign trade on the distribution of income', in Ellis and Metzler (1949)

Hicks, J. R. (1953) 'An inaugural lecture : the long-run dollar problem', *Oxford Economic Papers*, vol. 5. Reprinted in Caves and Johnson (1968)

Hirsch, S. (1967) *The Location of Industry and International Competitiveness*, Oxford University Press

A Selected Bibliography

Hocking, R. D. (1980) 'Trade in motor cars between the major
    European producers', Economic Journal, vol. 90
Houthakker, H., and Magee, S. (1969) 'Income and price
    elasticities in world trade', Review of Economics and
    Statistics, vol. 51
Humphrey, D. D., and Ferguson, C. E. (1960) 'The domestic and
    world benefits of a customs union', Economia Internazionale,
    vol. 13
Johnson, H. G. (1953) 'Equilibrium growth in an expanding
    economy', Canadian Journal of Economics and Political
    Science, vol. 19
Johnson, H. G. (1954) 'Optimum tariffs and retaliation',
    Review of Economic Studies, vol. 22. Reprinted in
    Johnson (1961)
Johnson, H. G. (1955) 'Economic expansion and international
    trade', Manchester School, vol. 23
Johnson, H. G. (1962) 'Economic development and international
    trade', in H. G. Johnson, Money, Trade and Economic Growth,
    Harvard University Press. Reprinted in Caves and
    Johnson (1968)
Johnson, H. G. (1965a) 'Optimal trade intervention in the
    presence of domestic distortions', in R. E. Baldwin et al.
    Trade, Growth and the Balance of Payments : Essays in
    Honour of Gottfried Haberler (New York : Rand-McNally)
Johnson, H. G. (1965b) 'An economic theory of protectionism,
    tariff bargaining and the formation of customs unions',
    Journal of Political Economy, vol. 73. Reprinted in
    P. Robson (1972)
Johnson, H. G. (1967a) 'The possibility of income losses from
    increased efficiency or factor accumulation in the
    presence of tariffs', Economic Journal, vol. 77
Johnson, H. G. (1967b) 'Some economic aspects of brain drain',
    Pakistan Development Review, vol. 7
Johnson, H. G. (1967c) Economic Policies towards Less Developed
    Countries (London : Unwin University Books)
Johnson, H. G. (1970) 'A new view of the infant-industry
    argument', in I. A. McDougall, and R. H. Snape (eds)
    Studies in International Economics (Amsterdam : North-
    Holland)
Johnson, H. G. (1971) 'Tariffs and economic development : some
    theoretical issues', in H. G. Johnson, Aspects of the
    Theory of Tariffs (London : Allen and Unwin)
Johnson, H. G. (1972) 'Notes on the economic theory of
    smuggling', Malaysian Economic Review, vol. 17. Reprinted
    in J. N. Bhagwati (ed.) (1974) Illegal Transactions in
    International Trade (Amsterdam : North-Holland)
Johnson, H. G. (1974) 'Trade diverting customs unions : a
    comment', Economic Journal, vol. 84
Jones, A. J. (1979) 'The theory of economic integration', in
    J. K. Bowers (ed.) Inflation, Development and Integration :
    Essays in Honour of A. J. Brown, Leeds University Press

175

Jones, A. J. (1980a) 'The theory of economic integration', in A. M. El-Agraa (ed.) The Economics of the European Community (Oxford : Philip Allen)

Jones, A. J. (1980b) 'Domestic distortions and customs union theory', Bulletin of Economic Research, vol. 32

Jones, R. W. (1961) 'Comparative advantage and the theory of tariffs : a multi-country, multi-commodity model', Review of Economic Studies, vol. 28

Katrak, H. (1982) 'Labour-skills, R & D and capital requirements in the international trade and investment of the UK : 1968-78', paper presented to the International Economics Study Group, London School of Economics

Keesing, D. B. (1966) 'Labour skills and comparative advantage', American Economic Review, vol. 56

Keesing, D. B. (1968) 'Labour skills and the structure of trade in manufactures', in P. B. Kenen and R. Lawrence (eds) The Open Economy, Colombia University Press

Kemp, M. C. (1962) 'The gains from international trade', Economic Journal, vol. 72

Kemp, M. C. (1967) The Pure Theory of International Trade and Investment (Englewood Cliffs, N. J. : Prentice-Hall)

Kemp, M. C. (1969) A Contribution to the General Equilibrium Theory of Preferential Trading (Amsterdam : North-Holland)

Kemp, M. C. and Wan, H. Y. (1976) 'An elementary proposition concerning the formation of customs unions', Journal of International Economics, vol. 6

Kemp, M. C., and Nagishi, T. (1969) 'Domestic distortions, tariffs, and the theory of optimum subsidy', Journal of Political Economy, vol. 77

Kenen, P. B. (1965) 'Nature, capital and trade', Journal of Political Economy, vol. 73

Kenen, P. B. (1970) 'Skills, human capital, and comparative advantage', in W. L. Hansen (ed.) Education, Income and Human Capital, Studies in Income and Wealth, Colombia University Press

Kenen, P. B. (ed.) (1975) International Trade and Finance : Frontiers for Research, Cambridge University Press

Kindleberger, C. P., and Lindert, P. H. (1982) International Economics (Homewood, Ill. : Irwin)

Krauss, M. B. (1972) 'Recent developments in customs union theory : an interpretative survey', Journal of Economic Literature, vol. 10

Krauss, M. B. (ed.) (1973) The Economics of Integration (London : Allen and Unwin)

Krauss, M. B. (1976) 'The economics of the "guest worker" problem : a neo-Heckscher-Ohlin approach', Scandinavian Journal of Economics, vol. 78

Kravis, I. B. (1956) 'Availability and other influences on the commodity composition of trade', Journal of Political Economy, vol. 64

Kreinin, M. (1974) International Economics : a Policy Approach

(New York : Harcourt Brace)

Krueger, A. O. (1974) 'The political economy of the rent-seeking society', American Economic Review, vol. 64

Lancaster, K. (1957) 'The Heckscher-Ohlin trade model : a geometric treatment', Economica, vol. 24. Reprinted in Bhagwati (1969a)

Leontief, W. W. (1933) 'The use of indifference curves in the analysis of foreign trade', Quarterly Journal of Economics, vol. 47

Leontief, W. W. (1953) 'Domestic production and foreign trade : the American capital position re-examined', Economia Internazionale, vol. 7. Reprinted in Caves and Johnson (1968) and Bhagwati (1969a)

Leontief, W. W. (1956) 'Factor proportions and the structure of American trade : further theoretical and empirical analysis', Review of Economics and Statistics, vol. 38

Lerner, A. P. (1936) 'The symmetry between import and export taxes', Economica, vol. 3

Lerner, A. P. (1952) 'Factor prices and international trade', Economica, vol. 19

Linder, S. B. (1961) An Essay on Trade and Transformation (New York : John Wiley)

Lipsey, R. G., and Lancaster, K. J. (1956-7) 'The general theory of the second best', Review of Economic Studies, vol. 24

Lipsey, R. G. (1960) 'The theory of customs unions : a general survey', Economic Journal, vol. 70. Reprinted in Caves and Johnson (1968) and Bhagwati (1969a)

Lipsey, R. G. (1970) The Theory of Customs Unions : a General Equilibrium Analysis (London : Weidenfeld and Nicholson)

MacDougall, G. D. A. (1951) 'British and American exports : a study suggested by the theory of comparative costs, part I', Economic Journal, vol. 61

MacDougall, G. D. A. (1952) 'British and American exports : a study suggested by the theory of comparative costs, part II', Economic Journal, vol. 62

MacDougall, G. D. A., Dowley, M., Fox, P., and Pugh, S. (1962) 'British and American productivity, prices and exports : an addendum', Oxford Economic Papers, vol. 14

Machlup, F. (1977) A History of Thought on Economic Integration (London : Macmillan)

Magee, S. P. (1973) 'Factor market distortions, production and trade : a survey', Oxford Economic Papers, vol. 25

Marer, P., and Montias, J. M. (1982) 'The Council for Mutual Economic Assistance', in A. M. El-Agraa (ed.) International Economic Integration (London : Macmillan)

Matthews, R. C. D. (1950) 'Reciprocal demand and increasing returns', Review of Economic Studies, vol. 17

McMillan, J., and McCann, E. (1981) 'Welfare effects in customs unions', Economic Journal, vol. 91

Meade, J. E. (1952) A Geometry of International Trade

A Selected Bibliography

(London : Allen and Unwin)

Meade, J. E. (1955a) The Theory of International Economic Policy, Vol. II : Trade and Welfare, Oxford University Press

Meade, J. E. (1955b) The Theory of Customs Unions (Amsterdam : North-Holland)

Meier, G. M. (1973) Problems of Trade Policy, Oxford University Press

Metcalfe, J. S., and Steadman, I. (1973) 'Heterogeneous capital and the H-O-S theory of trade', in J. M. Parkin and A. R. Nobay (eds) Essays in Modern Economics (London : Longman)

Metzler, L. (1949) 'Tariffs, the terms of trade, and the distribution of national income', Journal of Political Economy, vol. 57. Reprinted in Caves and Johnson (1968)

Michaely, M. (1977) The Theory of Commercial Policy (Oxford : Philip Allan)

Mundell, R. (1957) 'International trade and factor mobility', American Economic Review, vol. 47. Reprinted in Mundell (1968) and Caves and Johnson (1968)

Mundell, R. A. (1960) 'The pure theory of international trade', American Economic Review, vol. 50

Mundell, R. A. (1964) 'Tariff preferences and the terms of trade', Manchester School, vol. 32

Mundell, R. A. (1968) International Economics (New York : Collier-Macmillan)

Myint, H. (1958) 'The "Classical Theory" of international trade and the underdeveloped countries', Economic Journal, vol. 68

Naya, S. (1957) 'Natural resources, factor mix, and factor reversal in international trade', American Economic Review, vol. 47

Negishi, T. (1969) 'The customs union and the theory of the second best', International Economic Review, vol. 10

Ohlin, B. (1929) 'The reparation problem : a discussion', Economic Journal, vol. 39. Reprinted in Ellis and Metzler (1949)

Ohlin, B. (1933) Inter-regional and International Trade, Harvard University Press

Page, S. A. B. (1979) 'The revival of protectionism and its consequences for Europe', Journal of Common Market Studies, vol. 20

Panić, M. (1975) 'Why the UK's propensity to import is high', Lloyds Bank Review, no. 115

Pearce, I. F. (1970) International Trade (London : Macmillan)

Petith, H. C. (1977) 'European integration and the terms of trade', Economic Journal, vol. 87

Posner, M. V. (1961) 'Technical change in international trade', Oxford Economic Papers, vol. 13

Pryor, F. (1966) 'Economic growth and the terms of trade', Oxford Economic Papers, vol. 18

Raisman Report, Colonial Office (1961) East Africa : Report of the Economic and Fiscal Commission, Cmnd. 1279 (London : HMSO)

Ray, A. (1978) 'Smuggling, production and welfare', Journal of International Economics, vol. 4

Ricardo, D. (1817) The Principles of Political Economy and Taxation (London : Dent)

Riezman, R. (1979) 'A 3x3 model of customs unions', Journal of International Economics, vol. 9

Robertson, D. (1972) International Trade Policy (London: Macmillan)

Robertson, D. (1973) 'Multilateral trade negotiation', National Westminster Bank Review, February

Robson, P. (ed.) (1972) International Economic Integration (Harmondsworth : Penguin)

Robson, P. (1980) The Economics of International Integration (London : Allen and Unwin)

Samuelson, P. A. (1938) 'Welfare economics and international trade', American Economic Review, vol. 28

Samuelson, P. A. (1939) 'The gains from international trade', Canadian Journal of Economics and Political Science, vol. 5. Reprinted in Ellis and Metzler (1979)

Samuelson, P. A. (1948) 'International trade and the equalisation of factor prices', Economic Journal, vol. 58

Samuelson, P. A. (1949) 'International factor price equalisation once again', Economic Journal, vol. 59

Samuelson, P. A. (1952) 'The transfer problem and transport costs : the terms of trade when impediments are absent', Economic Journal, vol. 62

Samuelson, P. A. (1953) 'Prices of factors and goods in general equilibrium', Review of Economic Studies, vol. 21

Samuelson, P. A. (1956) 'Social indifference curves', Quarterly Journal of Economics, vol. 70

Samuelson, P. A. (1962) 'The gains from international trade once again', Economic Journal, vol. 72

Samuelson, P. A. (1965) 'Equalisation by trade of interest rate along with real wage', in R. E. Baldwin et al. (eds) Trade Growth and the Balance of Payments (Chicago : Rand-McNally)

Samuelson, P. A. (1967) 'Summary of factor price equalisation', International Economic Review, vol. 8

Savosnick, K. M. (1958) 'The box-diagram and the production possibility curve', Ekonomisk Tidskrift, September

Scammell, W. M. (1974) International Trade and Payments (London : Macmillan)

Scitovsky, T. (1942) 'A reconsideration of the theory of tariffs', Review of Economic Studies, vol. 2. Reprinted in Ellis and Metzler (1949)

Scitovsky, T. (1958) Economic Theory and Western European Integration (London : Allen and Unwin)

Sheikh, M. A. (1974) 'Smuggling, import objectives, and

optimum tax structures', Quarterly Journal of Economics, vol. 92

Shone, R. (1972) The Pure Theory of International Trade (London : Macmillan)

Singer, H. W. (1950) 'The distribution of gains between investing and borrowing countries', American Economic Review, vol. 40

Smith, A. (1776) An Inquiry into the Nature and Causes of the Wealth of Nations (London : Methuen)

Södersten, B. (1981) International Economics (London : Macmillan)

Stern, R. M. (1962) 'British and American productivity and comparative costs in international trade', Oxford Economic Papers, vol. 14

Stolper, W. F., and Samuelson, P. A. (1941) 'Protection and real wages', Review of Economic Studies, vol. 9. Reprinted in Bhagwati (1969a)

Stolper, W. F., and Roskamp, K. (1961) 'Input-output tables for East Germany with applications to foreign trade', Oxford Bulletin of Economics and Statistics, vol. 23

Tarshis, L. (1954) 'International price ratios and international trade theory', American Economic Review, vol. 44

Tatemoto, M., and Ichimura, S. (1959) 'Factor proportions and foreign trade : the case of Japan', Review of Economics and Statistics, vol. 44

Thirlwall, A. P., and Dixon, R. J. (1979) 'A model of Export-Led growth with a balance of payments constraint', in J. K. Bowers (ed.) Inflation, Development and Integration : Essays in Honour of A. J. Brown, Leeds University Press

Thirlwall, A. P. (1979) 'The balance of payments constraint as an explanation of international growth rate differences', Banco Nationale del Lavoro Quarterly Review, vol. 128

Thirlwall, A. P. (1980) 'The Harrod trade multiplier and the importance of Export-Led growth', paper presented in the IMF, September

Thirlwall, A. P. (1982) 'De-industrialisation in the United Kingdom', Lloyds Bank Review, no. 144

Tinbergen, J. (1954) International Economic Integration (Amsterdam : Elsevier)

Torrens, R. (1815) Essay on the External Corn Trade (London : Hatchard)

Vanek, J. (1959) 'The natural resource content of foreign trade, 1870-1955, and the relative abundance of natural resources in the United States', Review of Economics and Statistics, vol. 41

Vanek, J. (1965) General Equilibrium of International Discrimination, Harvard University Press

Vanek, J. (1968) 'The factor proportions theory : the N-factor case', Kyklos, vol. 21

Vernon, R. (1966) 'International investment and international trade in the product cycle', Quarterly Journal of

Economics, vol. 80

Vernon, R. (ed.) (1970) The Technology Factor in International Trade (New York : National Bureau of Economic Research and Colombia University Press)

Viner, J. (1950) The Customs Union Issue (New York : Carnegie Endowment)

Wahl, D. F. (1961) 'Capital and labour requirements for Canada's foreign trade', Canadian Journal of Economics and Political Science, vol. 27

Wares, W. A. (1977) The Theory of Dumping and American Commercial Policy, (Lexington, Mass. : Lexington Books)

Whalley, J. (1979) 'Uniform domestic tax rates, trade distortions and economic integration', Journal of Public Economics, vol. 11

Willett, T. D. (1975) 'The oil transfer problem and international economic stability', Essays in International Finance, no. 113, Princeton University Press

Wonnacott, P. and R. (1981) 'Is unilateral tariff reduction preferable to a customs union? The curious case of the missing foreign tariffs', American Economic Review, vol. 71